The Champion in You

The Champion in You

Kenneth C. Ulmer

DESTINY IMAGE® PUBLISHERS, INC.

P.O. Box 310, Shippensburg, PA 17257-0310

"Speaking to the Purposes of God for this Generation and for the Generations to Come."

This book and all other Destiny Image, Revival Press, Mercy Place, Fresh Bread, Destiny Image Fiction, and Treasure House books are available at Christian bookstores and distributors worldwide.

For a U.S. bookstore nearest you, call **1-800-722-6774**.

For more information on foreign distributors, call **717-532-3040**.

Or reach us on the Internet: **www.destinyimage.com**.

ISBN 10: 0-7684-2741-X

ISBN 13: 978-0-7684-2741-7

For Worldwide Distribution, Printed in the U.S.A.

1 2 3 4 5 6 7 8 9 10 11 / 13 12 11 10 09 08

Dedication

EVERYONE needs someone to see his or her hidden potential; to see the champion inside. I dedicate this book to men and women who saw the hidden conqueror in me and called the champion in me to come forth.

To my dad, George W. Ulmer, who often reminded me, "Son, you can do whatever you set your mind to do. Get something in your head and no one can ever take it away from you." My dad was a self-taught, play-by-ear, homespun musician. For many years he held down the bass section in the Gospel Chorus of Mt. Zion Baptist Church of East St. Louis, Illinois. He taught me to love music, from classical to country to gospel. He once wrote an arrangement of Psalm 23. The A-flat melody lingers in my mind to this day. He sent me off to the University of Illinois with the exhortation that I would have to work twice as hard as the class-mate sitting next to me, yet with the encouragement, "You can do whatever you set your mind to." My dad saw the musical champion in me. He was a champion.

To my mother, Ruth Ulmer. At this writing, she clings to life while grasping at shadows of reality. My sister Kathy and my brother Douglas take care of her. She is unable to read this book. She does not recognize me anymore. But she saw the champion in me. When I was ready to walk away from my first pastorate in frustration over the "stay-in-Egypt" mentality of some of the parishioners, she calmly taught me, "Son, most folk will do better if they know better. Maybe God sent you there to teach them." My mother helped me see my call and gift as teacher in the Body of Christ. She saw the teaching champion in me.

To the memory of Ms. Earnestine Triplett, who was my English teacher at Hughes-Quinn Jr. High School in East Saint Louis. She was the first Black person I had known who had traveled abroad. Every summer she would take a trip. One fall she came back and showed us pictures of the Eiffel Tower. As my eyes bulged with amazement at this Parisian architectural wonder, she looked at me and said, "Kenneth, you will go there one day!" When I stood for the first time at the base of that structural masterpiece, her words echoed in my ear. She saw the international champion in me.

To the wonderful men and women of Faithful Central Bible Church, who were among the handful of members who participated in my becoming pastor of this great church in 1982, in the spirit realm I humbly acknowledge that the Lord ordered our steps and brought us together to serve Him and His Kingdom. However, in the natural, God used you to launch an ecclesiastical journey that has defied the doubters, encouraged the faithful, and blessed the cities of Los Angeles and Inglewood, California. We have seen lives touched and changed by the power of the resurrected Christ. You have labored with me patiently and put up with sermons that were often too long and too shallow (and I am sure afforded you a time of slumber and rest in the pew, if not in the spirit!). Thank you for learning that it is okay to be saved and have fun. To Dr. Melvin

Wade, under whose anointed pastorate I heard and responded to the call to ministry. You saw the pastoral champion in me.

To Bishop Paul S. Morton, who consecrated me as Bishop in the Lord's church. He taught and inspired me to dedicate my life and gifts to changing a generation. He taught me to lead with vision and surround myself with other champions. He saw the Episcopal champion in me.

To the late Bishop Benjamin Reid ("Pop"), who was a gift to my life as I struggled in the far country of doctrinal doubts and theological confusion. He patiently walked me into the fullness of the Holy Spirit and opened my mind and spirit to new vistas in the spirit realm. He saw the spiritual champion in me. He also was the first Black person I knew who earned a Ph.D. He encouraged me to strive for academic excellence in my desire to study to show myself approved, a workman who need not be ashamed. He saw the scholar champion in me.

To treasured lifelong friends who validate the truth that you cannot always measure the depth of a friendship by the frequency of communication. Bonds that span decades become valuable pillars of character, and promote stability of integrity. To Willie Summerville, you allowed me to sleep on your floor and transformed your tiny apartment into an oasis of refuge in the desert of academia while we labored with "The Chief" at the University of Illinois. To Bernadette Officer, Mary Mask, Shirley Gray, Connie Wells, Esta Johnson, and Charlotte Ottley, friendships that transcend the years and miles between East Saint Louis and Los Angeles. You saw the friend champion in me.

To Dr. Jack Hayford and Dr. Lloyd Ogilvie, my prayer partners and co-laborers in the Kingdom. The times we spent on our knees praying for the shepherds of Los Angeles during seasons of unrest and discord on the City of Los Angeles were used of God to knit and glue our love for each other, our love for the Kingdom, and our love for leaders in the Church of Jesus Christ. You two precious brothers participated in my installation as President of The Kings College and Seminary for reasons that far surpassed the pomp and circumstance of a commencement ceremony, but bloomed out of a rare godly brotherhood. We have partnered in various preaching and teaching settings for many years in the common interest of pouring into the next generation of spiritual leaders. You saw and affirmed the academic champion in me.

To Dr. Larry Titus, who ushered in a new season of intimacy with the Lord and discipleship as a priority of ministry. You have been to me what Paul was to Timothy. You have walked before me as a father, walked with me as a mentor, walked behind me to push and encourage me. I have had many teachers, but not many fathers. You are the spiritual father in the likeness of my heavenly father. You prayed with me, prayed for me, wept with me, and wept for me during the most difficult seasons of an almost three-decade pastorate. You allowed the Lord to love me through you. You saw the leader champion in me.

To my children, RoShaun, Keniya, Kendan, and Jessica, who shared me with the world. My greatest fear was not to fail the church as pastor, not to fail the corporation as a CEO, not to fail the college as President. My greatest fear in life was that I might in some way fail you as a father. Your patience, your love, your support, your laughter, your tears and your prayers, and oh so many precious memories, have sustained me through those seasons when I felt like I was walking through the valley and shadow of failure. I am so very proud of all of you. You are my beloved children in whom

I am well pleased. I tried to do my best. Thank you for seeing the father champion in me.

Finally, to my wife of over 30 years, Togetta S. Ulmer. You shared your life with me when I had little or nothing to share with you. You were there when I had nothing but love for you. Together we have seen the faithfulness of the Lord on the mountaintops of excitement and the valleys of struggle. You believed in me when I saw nothing in me to believe in. You held me when I was afraid, prayed for me when I was weak, and pushed me when I lost confidence in myself. You saw the champion in me. You are my champion.

Endorsements

This book will unlock what God has destined each of us to be, and that is a champion. This isn't some quick fix, gimmick-filled book. Bishop Ulmer gives practical biblical principles that will inform you and help you to lead a transformed and empowered life. This book will change your life.

—Bishop Noel Jones
Pastor and Author

Kenneth Ulmer is one of my closest prayer partners, and knowing him as I do, I attest to this: *the man is real to the core!* The truths with which he inspires multitudes become real and livable because he is relating what he's learned and lived and proven.

—Jack W. Hayford
President, The International Foursquare Church
Chancellor, The King's Seminary

This is a very exciting book! It is a *can't-put-it-down* page-turner by one of today's most inspiring communicators. In *The Champion In You*, Kenneth Ulmer vividly portrays a divinely inspired, powerful biblical truth: God has placed within each of us a champion waiting to be discovered and released to be used for His glory and the encouragement of all those around us. If you want to get acquainted with this champion in you, this book will show you the way!

—Dr. Lloyd John Ogilvie
Former Chaplain, U.S. Senate

In a world that is filled with so many people who feel defeated or fearful, this word comes at a needy time. Bishop Kenneth Ulmer shares insights that transform the reader from the dismal to the dynamic. Take a read and watch the truths transform you until you emerge, undaunted, a champion for Christ!

—Bishop T.D. Jakes Sr.
Potter's House of Dallas

I would urge anyone who wants to know God's process for becoming a champion to read this book. People are facing challenges and situations today that can drain the goodness from their souls. Through *The Champion in You* you will be empowered to live life to the fullest. It contains new thinking on a biblical foundation that I applaud.

—Dr. Robert H. Schuller
Crystal Cathedral, California

Pick up this book and prepare to be changed! Kenneth Ulmer clearly articulates biblically sound truth on the topic of becoming the champion God desires you to be. Everyone is champion material and *The Champion in You* will bring out your best!

—John Bevere, Author and Speaker
Cofounder, Messenger International, Colorado
Springs/Australia/United Kingdom

Dr. Ulmer is one of the most strategic Christian leaders in the nation. His impact in helping people understand God's principles for life is enriching while remaining biblical. It is hard to overstate the impact Dr. Ulmer makes on tens of thousands of Christians every week.

—Dr. Mark Brewer, Senior Pastor
Bel Air Presbyterian Church, Los Angeles

This book is astounding. Kenneth Ulmer counters the critic's question of whether God wants us to be His champions with solid fundamental truths found throughout the Bible.

—Bishop Eddie L. Long, New Birth Baptist Church
Atlanta, Georgia

My dear friend, Bishop Kenneth Ulmer, is one of the most outstanding, creative preachers of our time. With *The Champion in You,* he has given us a creative biblical treasure that will not only capture our minds, but will also move our hearts toward a God whose heart is moved toward us. Reading this book will compel you to love God more deeply and to worship Him more fully!

—Dr. Crawford W. Loritts Jr., Author, Radio Host
Assoc. Director, Campus Crusade for Christ

In *The Champion in You* Dr. Ken Ulmer does what he does best. He slices through the confusion, misunderstanding, and misinformation about purpose and potential and then clearly and accurately explains the confirming Scripture.

—Robert Morris
Best-selling Author, *The Blessed Life*

What a blessing it is that Bishop Kenneth Ulmer has written a practical guide about how to step into God's purpose based on God's Word. Thank you, Bishop!

—Actress Angela Bassett and
Actor Courtney B. Vance

Table of Contents

Foreword

WHEN I think of champions, I think of courageous men and women who achieved great things in the face of great obstacles and challenges. These are men and women who know their goals, and the course to reach those goals. In many ways, their race is easily compared to our Christian walk each day. Champions take each day to build upon their previous day's successes or failures. They don't dwell on defeats or triumphs, but instead face each day as a brand new day and strive to reach the goal they so desire to attain.

We need more champions in the Body of Christ— believers who know their calling and strive daily to attain that prize which God has called them to. Many people in the Church are not building their lives off the eternal—His Word—but rather cultural thinking, tradition, assumptions, and emotional feelings of who God is. It's a scary thing to believe something temporal as being the eternal truth. If this is done, your foundation is faulty and setting you up for a sure fall. Champions don't build their lives in this manner. They establish firm foundations so that as they build toward their goals, they know their achievements will be sturdy.

We should search our hearts and examine the motives and intentions that drive us forward. Are you building your life for the eternal or the temporal? Are you striving to be an eternal champion, or one of this life only? God's ultimate desire is for you to be a champion in this life *and* eternally! But in order to do this, we must know what God has called us to and we must each day choose to follow the path that God has laid out before us.

I constantly see wise people of this world preparing for their future. It starts out with working hard in school to open the door for a good career. Once in their career they strive to purchase a house in order to build equity. They also develop some sort of savings. Some will take their excess money and invest, so it will work for them. All this is done to prepare for their future; they wouldn't want to be found wanting, especially when they hit their retirement years.

There is a parallel with those who are wise in the Kingdom. Their focus is not to provide a future in "retirement years," but an eternal future. They live with purpose and know their eternal destiny is being written by how they live here on this earth. This will provide for them a grand entrance into the Kingdom of God, rather than slipping in only with much of what they've done, burned up, and destroyed.

A while back, the Lord gave me a vision. I saw the champions of the Kingdom come marching into the city of God. They were parading through the streets of gold with multitudes of men and women cheering on the sidewalks. King Jesus was high up on a platform, visible to the great city. The faithful soldiers marched up the steps carrying to Jesus His spoils while the crowds rejoiced. In the vision it was as if the Lord was saying to those warriors, "Well done...."

Then the Lord asked me, "Do you want to be one of these soldiers who brings the fruit harvested for Me, or do you want to be one of these on the sidewalks cheering?" I determined more than ever before to make my calling and election sure. I was resolute in that I wanted to see a smile of pleasure on my Lord's face when He reviewed my life, not one of sadness, knowing the potential He had given to me was lost. I'm determined also to make this known to all who love Him in my generation in order that they walk with me into His great presence with His well-deserved spoils and see that longed-for smile of pleasure.

Will there be failures? Sure, but it is what we do with those failures that matters in the long run. Champions look at their failures as opportunities to learn and grow, and they use those failures to make adjustments in their lives to ultimately make them stronger. God will use your failures as a mighty testament to His grace, glory, and greatness. My prayer is that as you read this book, God would stir in your heart that you would be a champion in your generation. We need men and women to stand up and champion the cause of God in our world. God has great things for you, and you are a champion in Him!

—John Bevere
Author / Speaker
Messenger International
Colorado Springs / Australia / United Kingdom

Introduction

Discovering
the Champion in You

EVERYONE loves a champion. Even children seem to be born with an inherent desire to become their idea of a champion. When you ask children what they want to be when they grow up, their answers run the gamut: firefighter, doctor, lawyer, astronaut, president. Whatever their aspirations, children strive for their hearts' desires, truly believing they can accomplish anything.

Champions, however, are not born; they are *made.* *Webster's Dictionary* defines a *champion* as "a winner of first prize or first place in competition; one that does battle for another's rights or honor; one who shows marked superiority."[1]

Champions can be found in all walks of life. There are champion businessmen, champion athletes, champions of equal rights, champions for the homeless, champions for the rights of the unborn.

Past champions might include such names as George Washington, Abraham Lincoln, Henry Ford, Thomas Edison, Alexander Graham Bell, Marie Curie, Dwight D. Eisenhower,

Jonas Salk, Jackie Robinson, Jesse Owens, Mother Teresa, Aimee Semple McPherson, Amelia Earhart, Dr. Martin Luther King Jr., and countless others throughout history who achieved greatness.

Champions excel because they persevere; they go above and beyond the ordinary to achieve the extraordinary. We all know of people who put forth great effort to achieve their goals. There are also those who put in only minimal exertion. Those people rarely make it to the finish line, because they barely get off of the starting block. For many of them, this is because the thought of losing outweighs the training, the preparation, and the responsibility that comes with becoming a champion. Yet, the truth is, there is even a champion in those people; they have merely chosen not to make the effort necessary to pull the champion within them *out*.

BUILDING CHAMPIONS FOR DIVINE DEPLOYMENT

We each have an important race to run with our life. Even Jesus, the Champion of all champions, ran a race, focusing all of His attention on the prize set before Him: the salvation of mankind to the glory of His Father. Jesus never detoured along the way from the purpose marked out for Him by God. He stayed the course, He crossed the finish line, and He is now in Heaven, championing *you* before the throne of God.

Jesus is the ultimate example of what it takes for anyone to become the winner whom God desires each of us to be. The good news is that if you will faithfully and consistently follow His lead, you *will* become a champion.

Several years ago, a new team, Faithful Central Bible Church, took over the Great Western Forum, the sports arena that memorializes great champions such as Gail Goodrich, Wilt Chamberlain, Jerry West, Kareem Abdul-Jabbar, Elgin Baylor, James Worthy, Magic Johnson, and many others. We committed to carry on the Forum's tradition of being a house of winners and *building champions for Divine deployment.* Those five words describe the commitment that I have to help people from all walks of life—regardless of social, economic, or racial backgrounds—discover the champion in themselves.

All along our path in life, we are each given many chances to quit before we reach the finish line, or to slack off once we've achieved a certain level of success. In every field of endeavor, from the White House to the church house, men and women who have attained a height of personal achievement allow themselves to be defeated after being discouraged or disgraced by some indiscretion or misdeed. Then there are those who make it through life without a fatal blemish on their character and integrity, and rise to the status of champion.

Yet, to paraphrase the writer Menander, *The man who has never lost has never learned.*[2] Even through our failures, valuable lessons can be learned, and we can still emerge as champions.

God offers many opportunities to those who desire to learn and to grow into true champions, and He will never desert you if you will commit to putting in heartfelt, consistent effort at drawing out the champion already residing in you. Thus, there is nothing to fear and everything to gain in taking the steps to become a champion; for, as Joshua 1:9 says, "...the Lord your God is with you wherever you go" (Josh. 1:9 NKJV).

There are many factors that distinguish the champion from the average Joe or Jane. For example, merely questioning the average person's leadership abilities is often enough to cause them to quit. Or perhaps they are inconsistent in their efforts to overcome obstacles, resolve problems, and find solutions. What separates those people from champions is that champions are undaunted by seemingly impossible situations—not because they themselves don't fail from time to time, but because *champions don't quit.*

> True champions, when in desperate straits, lose their sense of fear. If there is no place of refuge, they will stand firm. If they are under relentless attack, they will put up a stubborn front. If there seems to be no help in sight, they will not give up.
>
> —*The Art of War*, XI.24 (paraphrased); Sun Tzu.[3]

The deep desire of my heart is to build and prepare champions for the Kingdom of God, to train and equip the average person to be released into the world to achieve great things in the name of the Lord Jesus Christ and His Kingdom. In these pages, you will learn how to be a champion in every area of your life. A champion in your relationships. A champion to your spouse. A champion for your children. A champion in your career. A champion in every possible way.

The heart of a champion beats within you, ready to begin setting a new pace. You *can* be an overcomer. You *can* be a conqueror. You *can* walk in victory. You *can* become part of an elite group that enters the winner's circle. To be anything less is to stop short of the very destiny that God has decreed for you. You do not have to be detoured by anything thrown onto your path. You do not have to be discouraged by any setbacks you may encounter. You have God on your side; He is with you wherever you go, as He promises throughout His Word, from Psalm 48:14 to Matthew 28:20.

God tends to use people who are unaware of the impossible to accomplish exactly that. If you assume that it's impossible for you to become a true champion in your own life, then it's time to make the effort and see what happens. Effort always trumps assumption. You are better off not realizing something is impossible and attempting it, than thinking it's not possible and never trying it.

The mass of men lead lives of quiet desperation.

—*Walden* (1854); Henry David Thoreau

In his first letter to the Corinthian church sometime around A.D. 56, the great apostle Paul summed up what it's like to stand on the winner's platform: "Death is swallowed up in victory. O death, where is thy sting? O grave, where is thy victory?" (1 Cor. 15:54-55). I believe our brief life here on Earth is all about legacy: What memory will you leave in the wake of your 70 or 80-odd years of living? If you are still drawing breath, then it's not too late to build the legacy of a champion. But the clock is ticking, so *carpe diem*,[4] for a great destiny lies ahead of you on a path paved by a God who loves you more than can be measured.

The Lord thy God in the midst of thee is mighty; he will save, he will rejoice over thee with joy; he will rest in his love, he will joy over thee with singing (Zephaniah 3:17).

In this book, we are going to examine God's definition of a champion, including:

- *What it will take for you to become a true champion,*

- *The attributes of a victor,*

- *Challenges that all champions face,*

- *How to stay in the game when others around you are dropping out or encouraging you to quit, and*

- *How to emerge a winner through the most difficult of circumstances.*

Let's get started on discovering the champion in you...

ENDNOTES

1. Merriam-Webster's Collegiate Dictionary, 11th ed., s.v. "champion."

2. *The Girl Who Gets Flogged*; Menander, c. 342-291 B.C.

3. Sun Tzu, born in China more than 2,550 years ago, is considered one of the greatest, most studied military tacticians in history. *The Art of War* is a compilation of his teachings, sayings, and ideas about battlefield tactics and strategy. As general of the army under Ho Lu (king of the Chinese state of Wu), Sun Tzu taught soldiers and officers what it takes to emerge victorious in battle—essentially, how to become a winner no matter the odds. Passages from *The Art of War* are presented herein not as exact quotes (as there are many and differing translations of his seminal, ancient work), but in paraphrase, in order to adapt Sun Tzu's battlefield success approach to the lexicon.

4. A Latin phrase meaning "seize the day."

Chapter 1

The Making of a Champion

I N April 1896 after having been dormant for centuries, the Olympic Games were revived in the city of Athens, Greece. Stands and stadiums were packed to capacity with sports enthusiasts and excited onlookers from around the world during this modern resurrection of the ancient games of Olympia. A shrill fanfare of trumpet blasts pierced the air, and hundreds of pigeons were released as the king called out, "Let the games begin!" Then came the procession of athletes. At that time, there were only about 250 competitors representing fewer than 15 countries. This was the beginning of what came to be known as the Olympiad of the modern era.

The ancient (and very first) athletic competitions began more than seven hundred years before Christ, in the craggy hills of the Greek city of Olympia. There was only one event at that first contest: a short footrace (which today we call a *sprint*). Two additional events, also footraces, were not added until more than fifty years later.

History records that Greeks invented what we now know as *sports*, where competitors vied against one another for physical supremacy in game-like settings.

The original site of the first games was a plain, ordinary field. Remarkably, it looks very much the same today as it did thousands of years ago. There were no seats. There was no stadium.

Thousands of spectators would gather to stand or sit, without shade or covering, in a huge clearing for five days to watch the contestants compete for supremacy. It was to this small town of Olympia that every four years, for more than a thousand years, men came from all over Greece, and eventually from cities as far away as North Africa, to compete in the various athletic and sporting events.

There is a profound difference between the ancient games and the Olympics of today. In the ancient times, the events were not commercialized, nor, surprisingly, was there much emphasis placed on the skill of the athletes. Rather, the original games were more of a religious celebration, dedicated to the Greek gods. Each day during the events, numerous sacrifices and prayers were offered to various gods and idols, chief of whom was Zeus.

Then, in A.D. 393, after more than one thousand years of Olympic competition, Emperor Theodosius (a Christian) decreed that all such "pagan cults" be banned (thus the reason for the time lapse between the ancient contests and the contemporary Olympic Games). By the end of the first century, the ancient Olympic Games had expanded to over three hundred cities. By then, Athens had become one of the crown jewels of the Roman Empire.

At the height of the popularity of these ancient Olympia games, roughly twenty years after the crucifixion of Jesus, Apostle Paul sailed to this very city on his second missionary journey. He would have come by way of ship into the harbor, and at the highest point he would have seen the Acropolis (the ruins of which can be seen to this very day).

And they that conducted Paul brought him unto Athens: and receiving a commandment unto Silas and Timotheus for to come to him with all speed, they departed (Acts 17:15).

In chapter seventeen of the book of Acts, we learn that Paul set sail for Athens alone, while Silas and Timothy stayed in Berea. When Paul entered the city—a great metropolis known for the arts, athletics, and philosophy—he strolled down its streets, passing by its great monuments and temples.

Athens had been the residence of scholars Virgil and Cicero, and the home of the great statesmen Pericles, Demosthenes, and Sophocles. The city was a melting pot of the greatest thinkers of the time—philosophers such as Socrates, Epicurus, Plato, and Aristotle. It was also the capitol of idolatry, populated by shrines, monuments, and statues dedicated to gods like Zeus, Athena, Aphrodite, Apollo, and Dionysus.

By the time he arrived in Athens, Paul's list of victories included Thessalonica, Iconium, and Berea. He had witnessed many signs and wonders and experienced God's power transforming him into an overcomer, a champion in the Kingdom of God. Imagine the clash of emotions this great champion must have felt as he witnessed the blatant pageantry of idolatry...

Now while Paul waited for them at Athens, his spirit was stirred in him, when he saw the city wholly given to idolatry (Acts 17:16).

As Paul walked the roads of Athens, he was gripped in his spirit as he witnessed the spiritual depravity and moral bankruptcy of the great city. The Bible tells us that Paul was "provoked" (see Acts 17:16 NKJV, NASB). One version says he was "deeply troubled" (see Acts 17:16 NLT). Others, that he was "distressed" (see Acts 17:16 NIV, NRSV). Yet another version says that the longer Paul was there, "the angrier he got" (see Acts 17:16 MSG). "Ticked off" would be a reasonable translation for today.

For Glory...to Whom?

The athletes who competed in the original games in Olympia did not compete for money. The contestants competed only for the glory of the competition. There was such a competitive spirit within the Athenians and the Greeks that, for the most part, the Olympic Games were a celebration of their competitiveness. The drive was to attain personal glory by putting up a noble and valiant effort. Certainly they wanted to win—every champion does—but the gratification of defeating another athlete was a secondary consideration.

In contrast, when we look at the life of Jesus, we see that, in all He did, He did it not to bring glory to Himself but to bring honor and glory to His heavenly Father (see John 17:4). For Jesus, God *was* the glory of the striving. The great champion apostle Paul said essentially the same thing in First Corinthians 10:31, that whatever we do should be done for the glory of God.

Real champions desire to live life in such a manner that God shines through in all they do, and all honor and glory goes to Him alone. If there is a personal reward to be given to us by our striving for God's glory, then *He* will bestow it upon us in *His* way and in

His timing. But the striving itself is sufficient for the champion of God. The purpose and the motivation of the Greek athletes, on the other hand, was to walk in glory, to compete in such a way that glory was reflected upon themselves in their striving to win.

Therefore, the question that we as Christians must ask ourselves today is not whether we are going to win, but *how* we are going to win. There are only two ways: either you are going to win in a manner that reflects the glory of the win onto God, or only onto yourself.

When I think of a true champion, I think of the movie *Chariots of Fire*, the epic film about two British runners who competed in the 1924 Summer Olympics. One man, named Eric, was a devout Scottish Christian missionary who ran for the glory of God. The other man, named Harold, was a Jewish student at Cambridge who ran for fame and adulation.

During one of the greatest scenes of the movie, someone asks Eric, "Why do you run?"

Eric responds, "I believe that God made me for a purpose. But He also made me fast. And when I run, I feel His pleasure."

No matter where we are, whether it's in a boardroom, a classroom, or an office, in every arena of life we need to feel God's glory, to live life in such a way that we feel His presence surrounding us and His pleasure flowing through us.

You know, Hannibal, how to gain a victory; you do not know how to use it.

—Maharbal (commander of Hannibal's cavalry)
in *The History of Rome*, XXII.51; Titus Livius

EVEN IN THE HARD TIMES

A friend of mine once went to prison for three years. Obviously, he messed up. He sinned—big time. And he knew it. While he was in the pen, I called him to try to encourage him. He was limited to just a ten-minute phone call…and this man spent eight of those ten minutes telling me how good God is! I was so overwhelmed I began to praise God myself, because although I have known other people who have been in jail, I never knew anybody like this man. I believe he had discovered the truth found in Paul's first letter to the Corinthians:

For ye are bought with a price: therefore glorify God in your body, and in your spirit, which are God's (1 Corinthians 6:20).

Sometimes it takes a devastating fall and a person to be knocked off his or her high horse to where he or she can see the feet of Jesus up close and personal. This friend of mine was humbled and he *got it*; he learned the lesson God hoped he'd take away from his experience. From then on, he was all "Glory to God!"

It's easy for people to talk about Jesus when times are fat and life is good. But when you're going through something rough and you're striving just to hold your head up, it's far more difficult. When we fall hard and fail big, it seems nearly impossible to praise Jesus Christ. But it's when you've been really broken that people can tell whether or not the Lord is truly magnified in your life. It's when you've been crushed and then repented that your real desire to glorify God is tested and revealed.

Champions give God *all* of the glory, no matter what. Your true master is revealed by the unveiling of a number of experiences: how much you desire to talk about God when it looks like you're about to lose your business; whether you remember Jesus when your spouse has walked out on you; what sort of testimony you have when everything around you—success, family, relationships, career—all seems to be crumbling at your feet; and how easy it is for you to glorify God when you're going through devastating trials and tribulations.

A CHAMPION IN GREECE

Therefore he reasoned in the synagogue with the Jews and with the Gentile worshipers (Acts 17:17 NKJV).

Apostle Paul saw that Athens had been overrun with idolatry. So he went to the synagogue and reasoned with the Jews and Gentile worshipers. The King James Version says that he "disputed" (see Acts 17:17 KJV). With his reasoning in the synagogue, Paul was giving his testimony, his witness.

Notice that Paul began his ministry in the synagogue, the house of worship, where the devout and pious Jews and Gentiles were. He was upset and grieved by the fact that the city had been taken over by statues and monuments erected to idols. Paul's first response to this travesty was *to go to church*, to where the devout people gathered. He was grieved, he was upset—so upset…that he *goes to church.*

Maybe he started with the folks who ought to have also been upset about what was happening in Athens; but there's no indication in the text that anybody was perturbed other than Paul. Maybe he asked, "Is there anybody here other than me who's grieved about what's happening in this city? Does anybody in the synagogues care about what's going on outside your walls? Does anybody in the pews care about what's occurring in the streets of this great Mediterranean capitol? Does *anybody* care?"

He must have been utterly baffled as to why nobody in the religious community seemed to care or even notice the spiritual degradation swirling around them. They had become the quintessential frogs in gradually boiling water, desensitized to the spiritual decay right under their very noses.

FIRST: CHAMPIONS STRATEGIZE

An important characteristic of champions is that they learn where the opposition exists. Once they know that, they then do these four things:

1. Gather information.

2. Devise a game plan.

3. Enter the game and engage the opposition.

4. Keep their eyes on the goal.

Let's examine them one by one…

First: Champions Gather Information

So he reasoned in the…marketplace day by day with those who happened to be there (Acts 17:17 NIV).

After Paul went to the synagogue, he went to the marketplace daily. The marketplace was a sort of town square, an open place in the center of a city for public gatherings. On one side were office buildings, complexes, and other smaller buildings. On another side, shops probably lined the street. At the other end may have been the civic and political buildings and offices.

From the moment he got off the ship and walked from the port through the city, Paul realized that something was seriously wrong. The church was not affecting Athens in a positive way. He started his inquiry in the synagogue as to why this was occurring. But the people in the church were unmoved and unresponsive to what was happening out in the city, so he went outside of the church to where the people were (people who were, by definition, not people in the Church) in order to truly learn what was going on.

If a church is not affecting a city, then the city is affecting the church. The enemy was busy at work in Athens and had obviously swayed even the Jewish leaders and Gentile worshipers away from Jehovah. So Paul went out into the city to locate the opposition.

Champions must always learn where the opposition is located. Know where your opponent is. One of the reasons the saints are so ineffective in cities today is because they don't learn where the enemy is.

SECOND: CHAMPIONS DEVISE A GAME PLAN

A champion must have a game plan, a flexible strategy that can be altered midcourse if necessary. After seeing the idolatry out in the streets, Paul went to the synagogue. Once he discovered the anemic condition of the religious people there, rather than allow his ministry and efforts to be limited to the inside of the church, he devised a plan to go out into the marketplace among the secular people. There, Paul disputed and talked and reasoned with the people he met as they walked or strolled by. He was effectively attempting to rouse the people from their complacency, to get them to wake up to the reality of the one true God and away from useless worship of their countless idols.[1]

THIRD: CHAMPIONS ENTER THE GAME AND ENGAGE THE OPPOSITION

You don't score points in the locker room—the game is played out on the field. It's the same way with the Body of Christ. The church is to be little more than a gathering place for champions to huddle up and regroup for a moment before launching back out into the world, where the battle rages. Yet, many people never get back in the game once they leave the huddle.

As Paul was out in the marketplace gathering information, talking and disputing with passers-by, he was invited to compete in the game, so to speak, when some local philosophers approached him…

A group of Epicurean and Stoic philosophers began to dispute with him. Some of them asked, "What is this babbler trying to say?" Others remarked, "He seems to be advocating foreign gods." They said this because Paul was preaching the good news about Jesus and the resurrection (Acts 17:18 NIV).

Key to the text is the passage, "because Paul was preaching the good news about Jesus and the resurrection." One version says the people listened to Paul "go on about Jesus and the resurrection" (Acts 17:18 MSG). Another version says "he was telling the good news about Jesus and the resurrection" (Acts 17:18 NRSV). The point is this: the substance of his message was focused very clearly on Jesus and the resurrection. In a city thick with stone and wood idols, Paul preached Jesus' life and resurrection power. He was bold enough to do so because he was a champion whose single-minded purpose was to preach Jesus and the resurrection.

In the town square, Paul talked about Jesus because his entire game plan was to preach a resurrected Christ. That is a bold plan that clearly honored God. Yet, out in the marketplace where he began to preach Jesus and the resurrection, the philosophers took notice and hustled him over to the Areopagus, the "official" arena for the presentation of thoughts and ideas:

Then they took him and brought him to a meeting of the Areopagus, where they said to him, "May we know what this new teaching is that you are presenting?" (Acts 17:19 NIV)

Remember, the Areopagus was a public area where the leading thinkers, councils, and philosophers of the city met together. It was where they settled disputes, debated, and discussed political and social matters. It was respected as a place where various philosophical ideas were disseminated and shared and debated—where the people would gather to hash out significant civic and social issues. To be invited to speak there implied that you were going to defend or declare your position on a fairly significant issue to everyone assembled. It was a place that was esteemed as the official location for the public iteration of *ideas*.

Not long ago I was in London, where I visited a place known as Speakers' Corner, which is located in the northeast part of Hyde Park. At Speakers' Corner, public speaking is allowed by anyone as long as the speeches don't violate any British laws. Any time of the day, especially on the weekend, you can find all kinds of people in this open court, talking about anything and everything. You don't have to have an agenda. You simply start talking.

The first time I visited Speakers' Corner, I didn't really know what it was. As I was walking through the park, I saw people standing around talking, and I thought that maybe something was wrong with them. But when I was told the significance of the place, I learned very quickly that not only do they talk, but they continue to talk until somebody stops to listen to them. They don't wait to start talking until a crowd gathers. They don't announce, "Ladies and gentlemen, may I have your attention, please." They just *talk*. There's something inside of them that they have a need to express.

If you truly have a word inside, its got to come out. There was something in Paul that had to come out: the message of redemption.

One of the reasons many Christians don't invite their nonreligious friends or acquaintances to church is because the Christians are ashamed to let their friends see how they worship. But if you want to walk as a champion, then you must come to a point in your life where you *want* to walk so close to God that you don't care who sees you or what anyone says about you. It is not your friends, family, coworkers, or neighbors who died for you and rescued your soul from hell. Every good and perfect gift that you now possess came from the Lord—who will never leave you or forsake you. (See Hebrews 13:5.)

There are too many secret saints and undercover Christians today who don't ever really enter the game. They value acceptance more than the price of telling the truth about the dangers of a life without Christ. All you have to do is look back on your life and see what the world has done for you, and you will probably realize that it isn't much. No matter what road you've traveled, there are times in your life that you can look back and realize that only the divine intervention of God Himself could have brought you through. Parents can point to the time when God helped them put a child through school. A single mother can see where the hand of Providence carried her through the loneliness and burdens of raising a child on her own. A businessman can remember when he was once down on his luck, and then God suddenly swung open the door of opportunity.

A dear friend of mine, national talk show host Steve Harvey, always sprinkles his show with testimonies about the goodness of God. He always closes his show with, "Don't forget to pray. Don't be too proud to pray." Steve says, "Without God you ain't got nothing." Steve Harvey could easily remain silent about his faith, but he is not an undercover saint (although he frequently declares, "Be patient with me, God ain't through with me yet!"). I love this man, not only because he is a friend, but because he is real about his relationship with God. He values the integrity of his faith more than the ratings of his show. He is who he is, and he knows who God is.

What happens with too many Christians is that, week after week, they go to church looking for the Lord to do something *for them*, while He is waiting for *them* to get off the sidelines and do something for Him and His children—because that "Matthew 25:32-46 day" will come when He separates the sheep from the goats and gives us our reward based on what we did while here on Earth (also see Matthew 7:20-24).

The most damage that the enemy does inside of the church is to *keep us inside the church*, while he continues to raise hell on the outside. Only by our actions and behavior out in the world can we carry on an effective battle against the enemy.

As a champion, in order to win, Paul set out to engage the opposition in Athens. He didn't spend much time in synagogues with people who had become so ineffective that they didn't go out and make a difference in the city. We too must stop spending so much time with church folks who are so righteous and holy that all they do is bow and pray and genuflect, but do very little when they finally get up and get outside of the church walls. Paul did not spend much time with them. He cut them loose and went into the city where he found people who needed the love and knowledge of God. He entered the game and engaged the opposition.

Ability to defeat the enemy means taking the offensive.

—*The Art of War,* IV.5 (paraphrased); Sun Tzu

FOURTH: CHAMPIONS KEEP THEIR EYES ON THE GOAL

Apostle Paul never lost sight of the goal of his life: preaching the redemption of mankind through the perfect sacrifice of Jesus Christ. The substance and focal point of Paul's message was always the person of Jesus. Athens was a city full of idolatry. As a champion, Paul boldly stood and proclaimed the resurrection power of Jesus.

When you go out into the world, into your "marketplace," what do you talk about? When you go to your office, what does your life communicate? When you take your children to school, what do other parents and teachers see in you? If there were a reality show tracking your life twenty-four hours per day, seven days per week, how frequently would those watching hear you talk about Jesus? Well, I have news for you: right this instant, as your eyes read these words, God is recording every thought you think, every word you speak, and everything you do, for playback at an appointed time in your future. He is not taking note to condemn you, but to use your testimony for His glory. He is not some cosmic big-brother out to get you. God is not looking for reasons to blast you, but reasons to bless you and to use you and your testimony to bless others.

Paul conversed with those in the marketplace because he knew that the Gospel of Christ was "the power of God unto salvation to every one that believeth; to the Jew first, and also to the Greek" (Rom. 1:16). He set out to preach Jesus in the midst of monuments erected to Zeus, Athena, Aphrodite, and many others. In the midst of this blatant idolatry, Paul was not about to contain the good news of the One who had met him on the road to Damascus and changed his life forever.

CHAMPIONS FIND COMMON GROUND

Once he arrived at the Areopagus, Paul began to give one of the briefest sermons he ever preached; yet it was extremely concise, prefaced with common ground, and guaranteed to get the attention of his hearers:

> *Then Paul stood in the midst of the Areopagus and said, "Men of Athens, I perceive that in all things you are very religious; for as I was passing through and considering the objects of your worship, I even found an altar with this inscription:* TO THE UNKNOWN GOD. *Therefore, the One whom you worship without knowing, Him I proclaim to you* (Acts 17:22-23 NKJV).

In today's vernacular, Paul would be saying, "Hey there, you Athenians. I see you are pretty religious people. The reason I know that is because you have religious monuments everywhere. In fact, I noticed walking down the street there that you even have an altar to 'The Unknown God,' whom you're worshiping without knowing. So let's start there, because the one who is unknown to you, I can introduce you to."

Paul was wise enough not to wait for people to come to where he was spiritually, theologically, or religiously; he went to where they were, to where their belief system stood. He found common ground upon which he could draw them into a comfort zone with him and then declare the truth of God.

The Greeks were a culture in search of supreme deity. They were searching for God but didn't even realize they were searching for Him. We know that because there were statues of gods all over the place. In their search for God, they overwhelmed themselves with a dazzling and distracting plethora of gods. They were so obsessed with "religion" that they even built an altar as an insurance policy, just in case they missed a god they didn't conceive of (and boy did they miss one!).

But the fact that the Athenians at least accepted God's unfamiliar existence is the crossroad where Paul met them to hand off the baton of understanding about the one, true, almighty Jehovah.

DESPERATELY SEARCHING FOR GOD

We too live in a time of lost people searching for God so desperately that they'll accept Him in just about any form they come across. And if they can't find Him in a form that they can readily grasp and easily fit into their own little box of ease and control, then they'll make a god in their own image. This craving for spiritual connection, understanding, and guidance represents an opportunity to Christians. Like the apostle Paul, we can introduce these people to the known God—the One they've heard of, but have yet to really learn about.

Once he had captured the attention of the Athenians, Paul then began to tell them about this "unknown" God they were being so careful not to offend:

"God, who made the world and everything in it, since He is Lord of heaven and earth, does not dwell in temples made with hands. Nor is He worshiped with men's hands, as though He needed anything, since He gives to all life, breath, and all things. And He has made from one blood every nation of men to

dwell on all the face of the earth, and has determined their preappointed times and the boundaries of their dwellings, so that they should seek the Lord, in the hope that they might grope for Him and find Him, though He is not far from each one of us; for in Him we live and move and have our being, as also some of your own poets have said, "For we are also His off-spring." Therefore, since we are the offspring of God, we ought not to think that the Divine Nature is like gold or silver or stone, something shaped by art and man's devising. Truly, these times of ignorance God overlooked, but now commands all men everywhere to repent" (Acts 17:24-30 NKJV).

Paul had cut to the chase: *Repent!*—time's up! Then he tells them why:

"Because He has appointed a day on which He will judge the world in righteousness by the Man whom He has ordained. He has given assurance of this to all by raising Him from the dead" (Acts 17:31 NKJV).

That was the abrupt end of Paul's official sermon to the inquisitive Athenians in the Areopagus. But something was missing from Paul's sermon to the assembled. Something was profoundly absent. Remember, Paul is the one who said in First Corinthians 2:2, "I determined not to know any thing among you, save Jesus Christ, and Him crucified." Yet, in this entire sermon at the Areopagus, he never once mentioned Jesus and His resurrection. Nowhere in his message did he talk about the cross. Here's why: Paul knew that in talking at the official place, the Areopagus, he was not talking to church people. He was not addressing synagogue members. He was talking to the thinkers, the philosophers, the officials, the hearers of new ideas. He knew that with this crowd he had to ease into the issue of raising dead people, by first laying a foundation of the "back story" of God.

Paul had discovered the Athenians' desire to become acquainted with a God they knew was somewhere out there. But he wasn't going to waste time talking to Greeks who knew nothing about a dead guy all the way over on the east side of the Mediterranean named Jesus until he initiated that connection through *God* (a God the Athenians were curious about, a God who is able to resurrect from the dead), which would then set the stage for discussion of a particular person God raised from the dead—a person named Jesus. Paul innately knew that first he had to find some common ground, to get a foot in the door, before dropping a whole new idea on them.

The mistake many Christians make is that they go to the world and talk church talk. When we talk with unchurched people in ways that we might communicate with our fellow Christians, what we have is failure to communicate. The unchurched person at your job doesn't know about anointing or the Holy Spirit or sanctification or the Trinity or factual specifics pertaining to Christianity. It can also be extremely ineffective to preach with an attitude of "accept Jesus or else you're going to hell." That "turn-or-burn" approach doesn't work on most people. If you go in shouting, "You all are gonna burn in everlasting hellfire and brimstone with weeping and gnashing of teeth if you don't get down on your knees and repent and accept Jesus right now!" you'll get run out of town quicker than a New York minute.

In his message at the Areopagus, Paul said nothing about the name of Jesus or the cross. He knew that the Stoics believed that there was something after death (they just didn't know what it was or who brought it about), and the Epicureans rejected all thoughts of any afterlife (living only for the "here and now"). It was the revelation of the message of Jesus that Paul was setting up to teach them. Out among the people strolling about the marketplace, he was able to tell the people about Jesus and the resurrection (see Acts 17:18) and to call the people to a point of decision to repent and start honoring this "unknown" God of all gods who is able to raise the dead. However, when he began talking to the civic leaders and politicians and philosophers assembled to hear him in the Areopagus, notice that the instant he said something about the resurrection, Paul lost them:

When they heard of the resurrection of the dead, some mocked, while others said, "We will hear you again on this matter" (Acts 17:32 NKJV).

Paul hadn't even gotten to his mention of the name of Jesus before they tuned him out and shut him down. They flat rejected him. The Epicureans made fun of him and mocked him. The Stoics condescended to him and patronized him. They basically said, "That's nice. But we'll talk about that later." They didn't want to discuss anything about any resurrection from death, and abruptly rejected Paul's attempted correlation. And they never had a chance to hear him out on the matter, because Paul never returned again to Athens.

The man and his message were rejected, and God never again sent Paul back to the Athenians.

CHAMPIONS SOMETIMES LOSE

However, some men joined him and believed, among them Dionysius the Areopagite, a woman named Damaris, and others with them (Acts 17:34 NKJV).

In the life of Paul, Athens can be considered a failure. Only a man named Dionysius, a woman named Damaris, and a few others believed. There is no record of Paul having established a church in Athens. He never mentioned it in any of his letters or epistles. Paul often returned to places where he had previously ministered, but he never returned to Athens. For him, Athens went down as a loss.

> "Winning is great, sure, but if you are really going to do something in life, the secret is learning how to lose. Nobody goes undefeated all the time. If you can pick up after a crushing defeat, and go on to win again, you are going to be a champion someday."
>
> —Wilma Rudolph, three-time Olympic champion

It's a fact of life that sometimes a champion will lose a round or two. Moses was a champion, yet he lost an entire generation. Jesus is a champion who had only twelve disciples, yet even He lost one of them. I'm a champion, and I've lost some...well, actually several. To tell the truth, I've lost a bunch! You may have as well. But you are no less a champion, because one of the identifying marks of champions is not whether they lose, but whether they *get back up and keep on going*. Being a champion is not about how many times you get knocked down. A champion always gets up one time more than he or she is knocked down, and at the end of the fight, is still standing.

My friend Donnie McClurkin echoes the words of Paul in his musical description of a champion. Pastor McClurkin and Paul ask the question: "What do you do when you've done all you can?" You just stand and keep on standing. Pastor McClurkin follows up with what is to some the autobiography of a believer. He says, "We fall down but we get up!" Sounds like a champion to me! (Donnie McClurkin: "Stand.")

Paul says we are to live life "in the Spirit" (see Gal. 5:25). Life in the Spirit is life in the power of the Spirit, and the power of the Spirit is resurrection power (see Eph. 1:19-20). Resurrection power is the power to get up and keep getting up. Resurrection power is God's provision for champions.

Your testimony as a champion is not based on your past failures or mistakes, but on what you did afterward. Did they defeat you? Or did they *strengthen* you?

Here is how we know that Paul didn't let Athens stop him:

After these things Paul departed from Athens and went to Corinth (Acts 18:1 NKJV).

Paul didn't mope. He didn't whine or grumble or complain. He moved on. He hit the road. For you, it may be time to move on to your next event. You may have messed up at the last one, but it's time to move on to the next. In the eyes of your world, you may even appear to be a failure who will never rise to the status of champion. But your final race is yet to come, and only you are the runner in your life's race, so *run*.

Every Sunday when I stand before my congregation, I may lose some. There are those who fall by the wayside for all sorts of reasons. Many are lost in their battles against the enemy, the challenges of everyday living, the fallout of bad choices, and their inability to bounce back after setbacks. In fact, after almost thirty years of pastoring, I am convinced that you can never grow a ministry if you are concerned about losing people. But God has always placed a Dionysius or a Damarius in the pews who realizes there's a champion within.

No matter where you come from, God is ready to take you into your next competition. He wants to fill you with the resurrection power of His Son Jesus Christ because He loves you so much that He gave His Son for you so that you would rise to become a champion.

Your personal history most likely includes a list of victories. Sometimes it's easy to look at our losses, but it is crucial that you deliberately recall your past successes as well. If you think about it, you can probably envision medals of triumph for different seasons of your life, maybe in business, or in personal relationships, or in education, or within your family. Bringing to mind the victories God has delivered into your life is the fuel that fires you to the next level. The constant knowledge that God is with you will spur you to accomplish what lies ahead. It is essential that you often take time to reflect and recall that you have tasted victory, and remind yourself that it *will* happen again.

One of my roommates at the University of Illinois was Hosea Harvey. Hosea was a civil engineering major. One semester he barely passed a test with a *D*. He came back to the dorm room understandably depressed, and I said something to him that became the motto of our room: "Hosea, you need to learn how to celebrate little victories."

He had barely passed with a *D*, but the victory was that in spite of his receiving a low grade, the class wasn't over yet—he still had a chance to redeem himself. And he did.

You may have done badly on your last pop quiz of life, but class isn't over yet. Learn to thank God for little victories you've experienced, the small lateral moves that can propel you forward, those incremental accomplishments that can continually steer you toward success. Every step in your life has brought you to this day. If some of those steps caused you to falter and fumble, then praise God you're still alive to run a new race—a better one than ever before, one that will give God the glory and you the victory.

We've all fallen at one time or another in our lives. Each one of us has been battered and bruised; many still carry visible wounds of battle. No one gets out unscathed. I've fallen down so often in my life that my knees are scarred. Maybe you didn't make an *A* on your last trial, but you're still in the class of life—you haven't quit. That's proof that you have a champion in you who has won some victories and still has many more ahead. The class of life isn't over. So show up at your next challenge knowing that it's your chance to score a win.

The important thing is not to count the number of times you went down, but the number of times you got back up. As long as you get back up every time you fall down, you'll be ahead in the game—and *that's* what makes a champion.

To muster himself to face the seemingly impossible—this may be termed the business of the champion.

—*The Art of War,* XI.40 (paraphrased); Sun Tzu

ENDNOTE

1. The Greek word for marketplace or town square, *agora*, is related to the word *egeiro*, which means "to rouse from sleep; to collect one's faculties."

Chapter 2

The Race of a Champion

I was born in a little town across the river from St. Louis, Missouri, called East Saint Louis, Illinois. East Saint Louis is a town much like Nazareth; a place about which it is asked, "Can any good thing come out of East Saint Louis?" (see John 1:46). Many might even dare call East Saint Louis a place filled with losers. However, one product of East Saint Louis would defy such a description: Jackie Joyner-Kersee, who once described the house where she was raised as "little more than paper and sticks." She came from a very humble background, but it is a testimony of the truth that where you came from is never as important as where you are going. Jackie was a champion destined for greatness.

After noticing an advertisement for a new track team at the local community center, Jackie decided to try out for the team. In her first competition she came in dead last. However, she would go on to become a champion with the Lincoln High School track team. In fact, she became a champion in track and in basketball while at Lincoln. She would eventually accept a track scholarship to UCLA. After the heartbreaking disappointment of making the Olympic track team only to have to miss the 1980 Moscow

Olympics because of the U.S. boycott of the games, she put her energies into playing forward with the UCLA basketball team, which continued sharpening her track skills.

This champion in the making would continue to face challenges and setbacks when she qualified for the 1983 world championships but was sidelined with a pulled hamstring. She would overcome the hamstring pull to participate in the 1984 Summer Olympics in Los Angeles but had to settle on the silver after missing the gold by five points. In spite of all these setbacks, including the untimely death of her mother at age 38, the champion in Jackie was still destined for greatness.

Jackie Joyner-Kersee is a champion. She was the first American athlete to win a gold medal in the long jump. On July 7, 1986, at the Moscow Goodwill Games, she became the first American athlete to win the grueling seven-event heptathlon, which she won by an astounding 200 points more than the previous record. She would go on to win three Olympic gold medals, one silver medal, and two bronze medals. She graced the cover of the September 19, 1988, edition of *Time* magazine as one of America's greatest athletes. She would set the world record four times, including her score at the Seoul, South Korea games in 1988.

Jackie Joyner-Kersee demonstrated what it means to be a true champion. In the face of the greatest obstacles—losses, personal tragedy, games missed due to politics, physical challenges—she never gave up on her quest to reach her goal.

It was the same with apostle Paul. His life was about winning souls, and though he only won a handful of converts to Christianity in Athens, the champion in him drove him to Corinth, where he would experience great success.

PAUL'S TRIATHLON

Do you not know that those who run in a race all run, but one receives the prize? Run in such a way that you may obtain it. And everyone who competes for the prize is temperate in all things. Now they do it to obtain a perishable crown, but we for an imperishable crown. Therefore I run thus: not with uncertainty. Thus I fight: not as one who beats the air. But I discipline my body and bring it into subjection, lest, when I have preached to others, I myself should become disqualified (1 Corinthians 9:24-27 NKJV).

After Apostle Paul left Athens upon being unable to persuade the Athenian intelligentsia of the salvation that comes only through Jesus, he moved on to the city of Corinth, where he established a church. After three years he left Corinth, and on his third missionary journey (around A.D. 55) while he was in the city of Ephesus, he received a letter that revealed that problems were plaguing the young church he had founded in Corinth.

By this time, the Olympic Games had spread to such a degree that many larger cities started hosting their own athletic contests. One such game held annually on the model of the Athenian Olympics was called the Isthmian Games, in the city of Corinth.

In his first letter to the Corinthians, in response to their questions and problems, Paul cleverly spoke in athletic metaphors, using terminology that compared the life of a Christian to that of a runner and a boxer.

Let's first examine the race of a Christian champion as compared to a professional runner....

How Champions Run

In the first Olympia event, runners didn't run on a track or a course as professional runners do today. Back then, there were two pillars placed on opposite ends of a long field. The runners would sprint from one end to the other, circle the pillar, and run back to the starting post. Sometimes they would run this two-way course back and forth up to twenty-four times.

The runners and sprinters became the superstars of the early games; and whoever won the first sprint had that particular race named after him for the next four years. The most popular Olympians today also tend to be the runners: Jesse Owens, Bob Hayes, Carl Lewis, Michael Johnson, Florence Griffith-Joyner, and, as we have seen, Jackie Joyner-Kersee. The names of many other modern track stars linger in the limelight, even decades after the athletes ceased competing.

In First Corinthians 9:24 (NIV), Paul asks, "Do you not know that in a race all the runners run, but only one gets the prize?" In other words, everyone runs in the race, but only one will win. Then he adds in the same verse that we should "run in such a way as to get the prize." Likewise, we are to live our lives in such a way that we are in it to win. Nobody gets in a race to lose. We are to involve ourselves with the vigor and determination and seriousness of really being *in the race*, going for the grand prize.

Champions take very seriously their involvement with the Lord. Even their church activities are not merely nice, weekly social gatherings. They don't make an appearance just to look good to other Christians. Champions are in it to be victorious, not mediocre.

Champions Are Distance Runners

Wherefore seeing we also are compassed about with so great a cloud of witnesses, let us lay aside every weight, and the sin which doth so easily beset us, and let us run with patience the race that is set before us, looking unto Jesus the author and finisher of our faith... (Hebrews 12:1-2).

Hebrews 12:1-2 teaches five things that Christian champions do that can be compared to professional runners:

Champions Lose What Slows Them Down

Champions Run the Race with Patience

Champions Learn How to Run to Win

Champions Stay in Their Lane

Champions Keep Their Eyes on the Goal

Let's take a close look at each of these attributes.

1: Champions Lose What Slows Them Down

Notice in Hebrews 12:1 that the writer describes the life of a Christian in terms of an athlete entering a stadium, surrounded by a "cloud" of witnesses. Many believe that this cloud of witnesses refers to the saints who have died and have gone on to their reward. They are those who can relate to what you're going through, and are now spectators in the stands, so to speak, cheering you on.

The King James Version of Hebrews 12:1 says, "Let us lay aside every weight." The term *lay aside* is symbolic of taking off clothes. It suggests a person who enters the arena wearing a long robe. Many garments back in those days were made of long, flowing material. If one were to try to run in this garb, the tucks and folds and pleats of the cloth would become tangled in the legs and cause the athlete to trip and fall. The athlete had to "lay aside" this robe before competing.

In today's Olympics, runners enter the arena in warm-up gear during opening ceremonies where contestants walk in wearing uniforms and carrying flags that represent their individual nations. Nobody runs a race in his or her opening ceremony uniform. Once it's time to compete, there are some things you take off and lay aside. It doesn't matter how cool your uniform looks or how warm it is, when it's time to get down to the business of the race, you have to take that stuff off and get serious about *winning*. That is what is meant by "lay aside every weight." It speaks of anything that's on your back that will hold you back.

This "weight" is not necessarily sin. It can also refer to having things in our lives that simply hold us back from doing our best. There may be things in your life that might not exactly be sin but are a drag on your forward progress, preventing you from being the man or woman of God you are called to be.

Most of us are intelligent and fully aware enough to know the things we need to lay aside. They may be cute. They may be designer. They may be coordinated. They may be cool. But if anything tends to hold you back from being all you can be as an ambassador of Christ in the world, then you'd better cut it loose and shed it if you want to become a champion.

We can never be the man or woman God wants us to be if we continue to hold on to what we know is negative or causes unnecessary distraction, even though it may not specifically be sin. It might be a relationship with someone who is holding you back. You might not be committing sin with this individual, but maybe he or she never encourages you to greater aspirations, or perhaps even disparages you. When it's time for the race, when it's time to train, there may be some things in your life that you're simply going to have to lay aside. There are things that you're going to have to learn to get along without. There are people in your life who you may have to walk away from. That is the mentality of a champion.

ALSO LAY ASIDE SIN

To the admonition of laying aside what weighs us down, the writer of Hebrews adds, "and the sin which so easily ensnares us" (Heb. 12:1 NKJV). This is more serious than the laying aside of mere encumbrances that could slow us down. This refers to plain old sin, the choosing of which will cause you to trip and stumble and lose the race with disgrace. It speaks of things that could be mortally dangerous to your journey. Thus, we must not only lay aside the heavy things on our back, but also sins that trip us up and can disqualify us from the race altogether, or nullify a win.

To be "tripped up" implies that you are not expecting a trap that lies before you—something that catches you off guard, usually in a moment of weakness or inattention, and causes you to stumble. It's the sins that you've been getting away with, compromising with, holding onto, petting and caressing, hiding in the closet, stuffing under the rug—sins that one day will spring out into the light and trip you up and destroy your integrity and Christian witness.

2: CHAMPIONS RUN THE RACE WITH PATIENCE

...run with patience the race that is set before us. (Hebrews 12:1)

Next is the instruction for us to run the race set before us *with patience*. I used to associate this with a lone runner in a marathon race. But marathon racing had not become that important or popular at the time this Scripture was written. The term actually speaks of a series of sprints that runners had to endure.[1] In other words, Paul was saying, *Hang in there!*—not with grim determination, but with hopeful steadfastness.

To "run the race with patience" implies that the weights and the sins that would try to distract or disqualify you from the race don't stop coming. Instead, you simply learn how to handle them, avoid them, go around them, and not engage them.

At some point in your life, you may have been in a position where you felt like everything was being thrown at you all at once. No sooner had you solved one problem when two more things broke out. When one person stopped attacking your integrity, two more jumped onboard and challenged your character. That's why the writer of Hebrews tells us that we must handle life with patience. You only gain patience through dealing with trials (which means you should hope that you already have patience and don't have to earn it, because patience is bred through the tough trials of life!).

The story of King David's early years is a tremendous example of the patience of a champion. In First Samuel 16:12-13, God told the great prophet Samuel to anoint David as king because God had become disgusted with Saul, who had turned out to be a selfish, lying king who often directly disobeyed God's commands. Saul was such a violent and unbalanced man that even Samuel feared him (see 1 Sam. 16:2).

Still, at God's direction, Samuel anointed the shepherd boy David, youngest son of Jesse, as king over the Israelites. David had been officially anointed, appointed by God, and was now king. Yet, because Saul refused to honor God's decision and step down, David patiently waited through twelve years of Saul's petulance, defiance, violent outbursts, disobedience, and attempted murder of him before finally taking the throne. First Samuel 17:15 recounts how David even trotted back and forth between playing the harp for the deeply disturbed king Saul while also tending his father's sheep—all while David himself was actually the true king (see 1 Sam. 17:15). Now *that* is a picture of the patience and humility of a true champion. Patience is knowing your turn will come and continuing to work for it, actively trusting God while you wait.

3: CHAMPIONS LEARN HOW TO RUN TO WIN

One may know how to win without doing it.

—*The Art of War*, IV.4 (paraphrased); Sun Tzu

In Philippians 3:13-14, Paul said, "forgetting those things which are behind and reaching forward to those things which are ahead, I press toward the goal for the prize..." (NKJV).[2] It is the picture of a runner coming in at the finish line and, at the last possible moment, thrusting himself forward, stretching his entire body ahead in order to force it across the line a fraction of a second sooner. This requires not only that the runner patiently run the entire race, but also to suddenly reach forward at that last instant to firmly grasp the victory.

During the 2004 Olympics, there was an athlete of around twenty years old who came in second during one of the heats, due to her inexperience. They knew she was inexperienced because, after the race was over, the broadcasters showed a replay of the race and observed that during the last few yards she had reached for the finish line *too soon*. She wasn't as close to the tape as she thought she was, and she lunged forward early. *She thought the race was over.* But in that split second of miscalculation, the girl next to her (who had never before won a race) zipped past her and took the prize. The girl who placed second missed the gold medal by a fraction of a second.

Champions learn: the race isn't over until it is over!

4: CHAMPIONS STAY IN THEIR LANE

The last few words of Hebrews 12:1 tell us to run the race that is set before us. The race set before us is marked out. Picture it as boundary lines that mark your lane.

Not long ago I was watching on television a race between several female runners. The gun fired and the young ladies took off out of the blocks. Not far down the track, one runner suddenly began to veer out of her lane. She ran in one lane, then another, and seemed to be almost drifting from one to the other. She wouldn't stay in her own lane. The trainers didn't know if it was the heat or what, but she appeared to have become disoriented and couldn't find her lane. She lost the race because she didn't stay in her lane.

The greatest revelation you will get in your life is clarity on what your lane is. Once you get clear about what God has called you to do, you don't have time to worry about it—you'll know what your lane is. You won't have time to step over into someone else's lane. You'll have all the blessings you need right there in your lane.

Some people miss the goal line because they were out messing around in somebody else's lane. If you want to be a champion, if you want to win the race, *stay in your own lane!* Know what career represents your lane. Know what job is your lane. Know what blessings are your lane, what husband or wife, what income level, what God has called you to do. The course God has mapped out before you keeps you from stepping over into another person's lane. The Scripture says that you are to run the race that is set out for *you*. God holds us accountable to run the lane He has marked out for us.

So many people miss the anointing of God's call upon their lives because they're watching and worrying about somebody else's stuff. Then there's another group that just doesn't like their own lane...

"I want *his* lane," they gripe.

"Her lane's prettier than my lane!"

"Look at what *he's* driving over there in his lane—I want that lane!"

God may be calling you to serve in ministry. He may be calling you to the mission field. He might be calling you to the pulpit. But many people back away from callings like those because they don't want vocations like that to be their God-ordained lanes. They don't trust that the Lord knows best and has their best, most successful, most peaceful and productive interests in mind, so they grumble about their lane and covet someone else's.

We can miss our destiny when we're too busy watching and worrying about what someone else is doing. Champions run the race *they* are destined to run, in the race that is set before *them*.

5: CHAMPIONS KEEP THEIR EYES ON THE GOAL

Looking unto Jesus the author and finisher of our faith; who for the joy that was set before him endured the cross, despising the shame, and is set down at the right hand of the throne of God (Hebrews 12:2-3).

In our final element of comparing the Christian champion with a professional runner, Hebrews 12:2 tells us to look to Jesus, the author and finisher of our faith. This means to *keep focused on the goal*. It means to run the race with your eyes fixed on Jesus.

In the race of life, champions don't keep their eyes out yonder on the finish line, because they don't always know when they're at their finish; only God knows that. You don't know how long your championship race will last. Just put your focus on Christ, and He will tell you when you're done. Follow His path for your life, and when you run, you will not stumble (see Prov. 4:12).

If you run your race of life in God's ways, (lose what slows you down, lay aside sin, run the race with patience, learn how to win, stay in your own lane, keep your eyes on the goal), then you will emerge victorious.

> "As I stand at the starting line, I know that somewhere out there is a finish line."
>
> —Champion runner John "*The Penguin*" Bingham

Don't Just Beat the Air

While the writer of Hebrews 12:1-2 describes the race of the champion in terms of a runner, apostle Paul describes the success of a champion in terms of boxing:

So fight I, not as one that beateth the air (1 Corinthians 9:26).

In First Corinthians 9:26, the word *fight* refers to the sport of boxing, as in an athletic event. Notice how Paul says not to box as "one that beateth the air" (1 Cor. 9:26). The phrase *beating the air* has several connotations. First, it's the idea of shadowboxing or using a sparring partner to practice and rehearse. Paul is effectively saying that he's not in this thing as a perpetual rehearsal. He's not just playing around. He's fighting to *win*. He is fighting for his *life*. He recognizes how serious this battle on Earth is.

Boxing in the early Olympics was nothing like the modern era with Muhammed Ali or Evander Holyfield. Men *died* in the boxing ring on a regular basis back in the early days of athletic competition, because there were no rules. Boxing then was bare-knuckle brawling. At the most, they would wrap strips of leather around their hands to keep their knuckles from being crushed against their opponent's cheekbones. There were no rounds. There were no rings. There were no corners. You fought until somebody dropped. For a man to die in the boxing ring back then was not uncommon, because the contestants were allowed to fight until someone hit the dirt and didn't get back up.

The implication of the text is that you're not just swatting at the wind; you're slugging your opponent. Paul is telling us not to fight on a whim, but to recognize the seriousness of the bout and *fight to win*. In this boxing match that we call the spiritual journey of life, the enemy may hit you sometimes, but you want the record to show that you got in some solid licks yourself. Many people have gone through a few tough rounds with life. They've cried, they've been down in the trenches, they've suffered; but they also got in some good, solid blows of their own. The devil even bats some champions around, but when the dust settles, he knows he's been in a scrap, because champions get some blows in too.

One of the reasons the enemy gets on some people's cases so often is that they haven't let him know who he's messing with. You need to let the devil know that you're going to be crowned the champ before the fight ever begins. Don't just psyche the devil out—get in his face.

Competition teaches us to rely not on the likelihood of the enemy not showing up, but on our own readiness to take him on; not on the chance of his not attacking, but rather on the fact that we have made our own position unassailable.

—*The Art of War*, VIII.11 (paraphrased); Sun Tzu

When I was growing up, my buddies and I used to walk past the railroad tracks on our way home from school. One day as we were headed home, some of the guys began to egg on my friend, Butch, to pick a fight with me. They kept antagonizing him and pushing him and shouting, "Go, man! Go get 'im—jump on 'im, man!" And they talked Butch into jumping on me, right by the railroad tracks—my own friend!

Well, let me tell you, we got into a knockdown, drag-out brawl. And after it was all said and done, I had some cuts and bruises. But mark my word, ol' Butch never jumped me again. Oh, he had me down in the dust, but let me tell you something, I got some licks in, baby! He knew I'd been there, I promise you. And we never had another fight.

Champions tell the devil, "I may lose a couple of rounds, but I bet you one thing: I'm going to get some nasty licks in on you. I'm going to show you the power of the living God residing in me. Shoot your best shot, but I plan on coming out the winner."

In order to defeat the enemy, you must be roused to anger against him.

—*The Art of War*, II.16 (paraphrased); Sun Tzu

You may go to church twice a week and lift your hands in praise to God, but as long as you draw breath on planet Earth, you're in the midst of a battle. You might go to work with a smile on your face, but if your marriage is falling apart and your kids won't speak to you, you're in the middle of a serious conflict that will have implications into your future. But God has given you the power to not only get your chops in and drive the devil out, but if you stick close to Him and seek Him for His way of dealing with things, then before your match is over, you will emerge as a champion and come out on top.

God wants us to learn how to rope-a-dope. When Muhammed Ali, the greatest world heavyweight professional champion boxer of them all used to fight, he would fall back to his corner as if he was getting his behind whupped by his opponent. He'd throw blocks and little jabs and taunt his opponent with, "Come on! *Come on!*" Then he'd fade to a corner and lean against the rope and let his opponent clock him so hard it looked like Ali was about to go down. But then the other guy would make a crucial mistake: he would get tired and begin to ease up on Ali a little bit—and the moment Ali appeared as if he were about to sink to the canvas, he would come charging off the rope shouting, "Is that all you got!" Then he would hammer the daylights out of the guy. Ali was like a Timex watch: "Takes a licking and keeps on ticking!"

Therefore take up the whole armor of God, that you may be able to withstand in the evil day, and having done all, to stand (Ephesians 6:13 NKJV).

In Ephesians 6:13, Paul encourages—indeed, *admonishes*—us to "stand." So *stand*, child of God. You may have tears in your eyes, but stand. They'll talk about you sometimes, but *stand*. You have to stand all by yourself sometimes, but <u>stand</u>. You may have some scars. You may have life-or-death struggles, but look at you: you're still standing right now. Sometimes you've got to tell yourself, "No matter what, I'm going to keep on standing!" God will bring you off that rope and you will do damage to the enemy in the name of the Lord, because champions learn that the harder they're thrown back on the ropes, the more they come out swinging.

Remember, in original Olympia boxing there were no rings, no corner, no canvas or hide flooring. You couldn't scurry back to your corner and get some hot tea, a little warm encouragement, and a cute Band-Aid after tripping on the nice mat. You couldn't get a cut man to heal you up real quick. You couldn't get a rubdown or a neck massage. It was brutal back in those days!

In life, there are always going to be times when you are out there standing all by yourself. It's times like these that you need to repeat the Word of God to yourself:

"I shall not die, but live and declare the works of the Lord!" (see Ps. 118:17).

"No weapon formed against me shall prosper!" (see Isa. 54:17).

"Thanks be to God, who gives me victory through Jesus Christ. I will be steadfast, immovable, always abounding in the work of the Lord, knowing that my labor is not in vain in the Lord!" (see 1 Cor. 15:57-58).

"He who is in me is greater than he who is in the world!" (see 1 John 4:4).

Then come off the ropes swinging and open up on the enemy, and you'll get your victory because you are a champion.

THE CHAMPION IN YOU

The wise champion imposes his will on the enemy, but does not allow the enemy's will to be imposed upon him.

—*The Art of War*, VI.2 (paraphrased); Sun Tzu

Off with the Gloves

For we wrestle not against flesh and blood, but against principalities, against powers, against the rulers of the darkness of this world, against spiritual wickedness in high places (Ephesians 6:12).

Due to the high priority placed on sporting events in Greece, apostle Paul used many descriptive analogies to compare the life of the Christian with professional athletes, such as runners and boxers. In Ephesians 6:12, Paul uses the word *wrestle*. As in boxing, wrestling was a sport with no real rules. You could essentially do whatever you had to do to hold on and stay in the match. Later, a combination of wrestling and boxing was developed called *pankration*, in which you could kick, hit, or choke your opponent. One of the most popular things that combatants would do in pankration was to break the fingers of their opponents, not only to cause great pain and incapacitate them, but also to frighten and intimidate other athletes who would hear the bones crack.

As in boxing, the competitors fought until someone quit, passed out, or died. The one remaining at the end of the bout was ruled the champion.

Christian champions today are involved in three different types of wrestling matches:

WE WRESTLE WITH OURSELVES

In First Corinthians 9:27 Paul says, "I beat my body" (NIV) or "discipline my body" (NKJV) in order to "bring it into subjection" in accordance with God's will (see 1 Cor. 9:27 NIV, NKJV). The reason for this is that often our greatest opponent is ourselves, so we have to continually bring our thoughts and behavior back into line with God's Word.

While driving and listening to the radio one day, my attention was captured by a song that musically dramatized spiritual warfare. I was surprised and impressed when the "hook line" of the song said, "Hide me from the enemy; even if the enemy is inside me." The artist, Reverend Bruce Parham, had musically captured the exhortation of Paul (Bruce Parham, "Hide Me").

WE WRESTLE WITH SATAN

Second, as Paul reminds us in Ephesians 6:12, "our struggle is not against flesh and blood, but against the rulers, against the powers, against the world forces of this darkness, against the spiritual forces of wickedness in the heavenly places" (Eph. 6:12 NASB). This means we're not only wrestling with ourselves, but we're also wrestling with the spirit realm, where demons are assigned as messengers to thwart and short-circuit God's call on our lives. When our wrestling match is in the spirit realm, as Paul says in Ephesians 6:13, we must take up the whole armor of God, which means that we overcome the enemy by the provision

THE CHAMPION IN YOU

of the Word, by steadfast faith in God, and by the power of the Holy Spirit within us (see Eph. 6:13).

WE WRESTLE WITH GOD

The third wrestling match is the real bear. It's the one that can come in times of desperation. It's when you wrestle with God, like Jacob did in Genesis 32:24. Jacob was in both a literal and a spiritual wrestling match—with himself and with God. He was actually running away after God had told him in Genesis 32:9 to go back to his country and his relatives, where God would bless him (see Gen. 32:9). But Jacob knew he had been "deceitful" and was a "supplanter" (which is what the name *Jacob* means). He had conned his brother Esau out of his inheritance rights as firstborn son and was fleeing for his life. God basically told Jacob, "Go back and I'll bless you." But Jacob essentially replied, "No way!—they're going to kill me!" However, when he realized it was God he was wrestling with, he stopped his attitude of running, latched onto God, and reminded Him of His promise to bless Abraham, Isaac, and their offspring. (See Genesis 32.)

Jacob didn't want to lose his full inheritance, and he wanted to make sure his past sins wouldn't prevent him from receiving God's promise, so he insisted that God assure him that He would follow through on His Word. "I will not let You go unless You bless me!" Jacob cried out in Genesis 32:26 (Gen. 32:26 NKJV). Talk about bold! In spite of Jacob's character flaws, God commended Jacob's tenacity, blessed him, and even gave him a new name, Israel, which means, "He strives with God," or, "May God persevere."

Your name shall no longer be called Jacob, but Israel; for you have struggled with God and with men, and have prevailed (Genesis 32:28 NKJV).

If it becomes necessary, champions have no qualms about righteous wrestling with God. It worked for Jacob. From master manipulator to humble servant, Jacob was now a true champion in the eyes of God. That competition—his struggle with God—revealed Jacob's character. In the Kingdom of God, things are often upside down. In order to go up, we must go down. Humble yourself and you shall be exalted (see James 4:10). If you want to be strong, you must become weak (see 2 Cor. 12:10). If you want to have, you must give (see Luke 6:38). And Jacob teaches us that if you want to win, you must surrender to the power of God. You let go of everything else and you hold on to God.

"Sports do not build character; they reveal it."

—John Wooden,
coach of ten NCAA basketball championship teams

HOLD ON FOR THE BLESSING

Once Jacob realized who had His hand on him, instead of fighting to get away, he started fighting to hold on. Your real blessing is when you hold on to God, because in this match of life, holding is permissible. God may be trying to bless you, so don't try to break loose and run—hold on to Him and don't let go.

Jacob said, "I won't let you go until you bless me." I say to you, "Hold on, child of God; your blessing is on the way!"

Hold on and you will get your deliverance. Hold on till the storm passes over. Be bold enough to tell God, "Lord, I know I've sinned. I'm a sinner. But I love You, Lord, and I'm not going to let You go until You bless me. I'm not going to let You go until you bless my home. I'm not going to let You go until you bless my finances. I'm not going to let You go until you bless my testimony, my marriage, my children. Oh Lord, I am not asking from a position of arrogance or demanding from a position of entitlement, but I am holding on because without You I can do nothing. I am holding on because I need Your forgiveness. I need Your grace. I need Your mercy. I need Your power."

Champions hold on. Your tussle with the Holy Spirit may just be an indication that your blessing is on the way. Hold onto the belief that God has a blessing with your name on it.

Someone has been trying to knock you down, *but hold on*.

You get weary sometimes, *but keep holding on*.

People are talking behind your back, *but hold on*.

You might not have a dollar in your pocket, but *keep holding on*.

People may have scandalized your name, *but hold on*.

You might have some scars, *but still hold on*.

You may have to cry, *but hold on*; the storm will pass by.

The match is not over. The best match of your life is being written right now.

When Jacob received his blessing, God touched him in his hip; and from that time on, Jacob walked with a limp. Everyone knew something was different about him, because Jacob was changed both physically and spiritually.

You can exalt God even when you limp. In fact, it's our limp from wrestling with God that keeps us humble. Our limp is a constant reminder to seek His face. Our limp makes us turn to our best chance of victory: Jesus Christ.

I've seen boxing and wrestling matches where a guy was being beaten so badly he just draped himself around his adversary and clung to him and swayed back and forth, barely able to maintain vertical. What I realized was that while he was holding on and being flung back and forth, something in him was being revived. There have been times in my life when God was all I had to hold on to, times when I found myself like Jacob, in a wrestling match with God—who was trying only to accomplish something in my life and bless me, all while I was striving against Him. I cannot tell you how many times I found myself trying to run away from God, who just wanted to draw me close to Him. The frustration, the confusion, the pain, and the discouragement were overwhelming within me. And all the while, He was attempting to pull me out of something and take me to a better place and make me a champion. And it dawned on me that I was resisting and pulling away while God was trying to bless me and draw me near! So I changed my strategy. Instead of pulling away from Him, I began to hold on to Him and allow Him to refresh, renew, and bless me.

I want to encourage you that if you've done everything you can to stand, then *keep on standing.* Shift your strategy. Instead of pulling away from Him, clutch Him tightly. Hold on—*and refuse to let Him go!*

> If God's commands are habitually followed, the champion will be well-disciplined; if not, his discipline will falter.

> —*The Art of War*, IX.44 (paraphrased); Sun Tzu

One day I was driving by a Honda dealership in Inglewood, a small city adjacent to Los Angeles. They were drawing attention to a huge car sale by pumping air into a large balloon in the shape of a man that was blowing back and forth in the wind from the air gushing into it. Its arms, legs, and head were flapping every which way. Every now and then it looked like it was about to go flat, but air kept billowing into it, and pretty soon the flailing man was flying high again. Then traffic would slow up and there was less of a draft, and he would start to deflate and would winnow down again. This big, smiling, arm-flapping man never stopped going up and down, up and down.

God knows when you're down. I've been down. We've all been down. But I promise you, He is breathing the breath of His Spirit into you. If you will just discipline yourself to hold on, if you will just tell that old devil, "I'm not going down today! You do whatever you've got to do, but I am going to stand right here until my change comes," then you will win the race of the champion.

> "No athlete is crowned but in the sweat of his brow."

> —Saint Jerome, Letter 14

ENDNOTES

1. The Greek word for patience is *hupomone*, which means "to abide with hope-filled endurance."

2. The Greek word for reach is *epekteinomai*, which means "to stretch forward."

Chapter 3

Champions Prepare

"In football and in business, preparation precedes performance."

—Bill Walsh, professional football coach

IN any competition, whether it's between athletes, businessmen, or simply in the race of life, the champion must be in good physical, mental, and spiritual condition. For the champion, this preparation begins far from the limelight, long before there are accolades or cheers or success.

We look to the Book of Romans to begin our investigation of how a champion prepares to succeed:

> I beseech you therefore, brethren, by the mercies of God, that you present your bodies a living sacrifice, holy, acceptable to God, which is your reasonable service. And do not be conformed to this world, but be transformed by the renewing of your mind, that you may prove what is that good and acceptable and perfect will of God (Romans 12:1-2 NKJV).

Not being conformed to the world, but being transformed by the renewing of the mind is the idea of metamorphosis of one's thought process. That is, our mind must be reprogrammed to God's way of doing things, or else we will be confined to the world's way of thinking and conformed to that image rather than to the image of God. The word *conformed* in Romans 12:2 refers to being squeezed into a mold. In other words, don't let the world squeeze you into its mold or its mentality. Don't live your life according to the standards of the cultures around you.

In brief, this is what the "things of God" consist of:

Whatever things are true, whatever things are noble, whatever things are just, whatever things are pure, whatever things are lovely, whatever things are of good report, if there is any virtue and if there is anything praiseworthy—meditate on these things (Philippians 4:8 NKJV).

When our mind is transformed, a change begins to take place so that our definition of being a champion, of being successful, of achieving in the world, comes into line with God's Word, which directs us to focus on the things that are true, noble, just, pure, lovely, of good report, of virtue, and praiseworthy.

Once a person's mind has been transformed by God's Word, he or she is ready to act on that transformation—that *preparation*—as the example of Joshua shows:

After the death of Moses the servant of the LORD, it came to pass that the LORD spoke to Joshua the son of Nun, Moses' assistant, saying: "Moses My servant is dead. Now therefore, arise, go over this Jordan, you and all this people, to the land which I am giving to them—the children of Israel (Joshua 1:1-2 NKJV).

In Joshua 1:1-2, God called Joshua to lead the people of Israel into the Promised Land. That was Joshua's divine destiny, and God laid out a plan for Joshua to follow so he could fulfill that destiny.

The Joshua 1 passage lays out three key points that are crucial to the training and preparation of a champion:

FIRST: BE READY TO MOVE FROM ONE SEASON TO ANOTHER

Champions are ready and willing to change with the seasons. With the death of Moses came the end of a wilderness season and the beginning of a possession season. There was a changing of the guard. Now it was Joshua's turn to rise to the position of leader of the nation of Israel.

In Joshua 1:1-2, God told Joshua that Moses was dead, that the season of Moses had come to an end. Joshua was now to arise and lead the people into the Promised Land. Joshua's basic instructions were, "Get your eyes off of Moses and go. Now it's your turn. Take the people to the land."

Later in chapter 1, God tells Joshua that if he stays faithful to do what God tells him, the Israelites will be successful in taking the land. There is continuity to God's methodology:

1. Things have changed: Moses is dead.

2. We're going with a new plan: Joshua will lead the people into Canaan.

3. Do it God's way: It will all work out fine.

There is a short but inspiring book titled *Who Moved My Cheese?* that talks about how to transition from one season to the next. It's about handling change. *Who Moved My Cheese?* is the story of two mice and two people and the challenges they face when their worlds are upset by change. They live in a maze where they aspire to achieve in life, a concept that is represented in the story by cheese. The moral of the story is that we have to be prepared for change and ready to move forward when the old ways end or are changed.[1]

Moses was a great leader who accomplished many amazing things. But now there was a changing of the guard. The old ways of Moses no longer applied. There was a new leader (Joshua) who possessed different leadership qualities and management styles. You can see the differences when you compare the parting of the Red Sea by Moses and the parting of the Jordan River by Joshua. Moses stretched out his rod over the Red Sea, thus parting it so that the Israelites could cross over. Joshua sent forth the priests with the Ark of the Covenant into the Jordan, which then parted, enabling the people to pass through (see Joshua 3:15-17).[2]

Joshua was a champion who did not hesitate to roll with the new season that was suddenly thrust upon him by God.[3]

SECOND: FIND YOUR MENTOR

The second revelation is this: if you want to become a champion, get into relationship with a champion who will mentor you, someone who is where you want to go and who has learned what you need to learn.

As the assistant to Moses, Joshua was effectively mentored by the great prophet:

Then the Lord said to Moses, "Come up to Me on the mountain and be there; and I will give you tablets of stone, and the law and commandments which I have written, that you may teach them." So Moses arose with his assistant Joshua, and Moses went up to the mountain of God (Exodus 24:12-13 NKJV).

Connect with a champion who knows something about success. Moses led the people from Egypt right to the door of Canaan. Moses had opposition. Moses went through trials. He suffered discouragement. Yet his love for Jehovah, and his desire to do all that the Lord had for him to do, helped him push through his trials, all the way to the Jordan River, within sight of the Promised Land. That is a champion and a success in God's eyes.

Moses dealt with countless complaints from the Israelites, murmurings against him (even from his sister Miriam and brother Aaron, as told in Numbers 12:1), and the peoples' refusal to consistently honor the Almighty and put Him first. They wanted to turn back to Egypt and abandon their pursuit of the land of milk and honey. They whined about the manna from heaven. An entire generation died or was killed as a result of all this whining and grumbling. But Moses didn't quit.

In steadfastly standing by and assisting Moses, Joshua had hooked up with somebody who knew something about being a champion. To become a champion yourself, get into a relationship of responsibility and accountability with someone who is a

champion, a Christian who is living his or her life by the Book—
a mentor who will pour him or herself into your life.

THIRD: BE READY WHEN IT'S YOUR TIME

The enlightened champion lays his plans well ahead.

—*The Art of War*, XII.16 (paraphrased); Sun Tzu

Champions understand the idea of *preparation*. Joshua spent
years in training and development under the tutelage of Moses;
and when his time came to lead the Israelites, he was ready. He'd
done his homework, he'd learned his lessons well; he was prepared
to part the Jordan and march his people across the river and into
the Promised Land.

When Moses died, God basically told Joshua, "The end result
of the relationship I had you in with Moses is at hand. It is now
your turn to lead My people" (see Josh. 1:1-2).

A dear friend of mine from South Africa once told me, "We
have a major problem in our society here in South Africa. There are
all kinds of opportunities for advancement and success. But our
problem now is that while all of the doors are open, there are few
of us who are ready to walk through them, because of all of the
decades of revolution and apartheid."

The cry of the revolution had been "Freedom now, freedom
now! Education later! Freedom now, freedom now!" But when
apartheid ended during F.W. de Klerk's presidency, and the South
African people won their struggle for freedom, the new leaders
realized that a severe vacuum had developed during apartheid. The
doors of opportunity were swinging open for the people, but they

weren't trained or well equipped enough to step through the doors. Because of the areas of massive need required to rebuild society, people came from all over the world to fill the void. They came from Asia, America, Australia, and Europe to fill in the gaps because the South African people weren't prepared. Abundant opportunities quickly arose, but many indigenous people were unable to participate in the bounty that was becoming available all around them.[4]

There are champions all over South Africa who are stepping through the doors of opportunity because they are prepared. They saw it coming and they got ready. Some studied in America and Europe, even while they were in exile. They knew their time was coming, and when it came, they would be ready.

When the doors of opportunity swing open, champions are prepared to step in. People can bellyache all they want when they're on the bench, but when they get in the game, they'd better run that ball. You can sit back and complain about how this person is running her company and how that guy is messing up that job, but when you get the opportunity, you better *produce*. When the ball is snapped and the quarterback steps back into the pocket and scans his receivers, each one of them had better be nearing the mark, ready to spin and catch that ball—whether it's thrown to him or not. Champions are ready before the snap.

Most of us want to stand on top of the mountain of success, but few want to spend the time in the valley of preparation, which is what it takes to get to the mountaintop. When you see Sylvester Stallone celebrating on the top of the steps in the movie *Rocky*, don't forget all the lonely nighttime runs and hitting practice sessions in the meat freezer that he went through before he reached the top of those steps. Too many Christians don't understand the value of sweating their way toward the top, slogging up the mountain, and hacking through the dense underbrush—where champions prepare themselves, where they pay their dues, where they hone their chops, where they get the blade sharp. Contrary to the song in *Dreamgirls*, you can't "fake your way to the top."

The problem with many people who want to be champions nowadays is that they're looking for a shortcut. Everybody wants a quick and easy way to the top. Everybody has a hustle and a scam. But the principle of Joshua is that you stand your turn, you do your homework, you seek God's direction, you get prepared. And when your time comes, you step up to the plate and aim for the backfield flood lamps, because you're ready to knock that ball out of the park.

"You must learn to maximize the moment."

—T.D. Jakes

When the opportunity arose for Faithful Central Bible Church to purchase the Great Western Forum, we had a decision to make right then, because the opportunity was not going to wait on us. We did not have time to spend a year in consideration and investigation. But God had sovereignly prepared our church, so that when the opportunity came, we were ready. We'd done our homework.

The first meeting we had with the various parties involved told us it could not be done—no local church was going to purchase the entire mighty Great Western Forum, which had been home to the invincible Los Angeles Lakers professional basketball club. But before we even considered moving into the Forum, we already had experience believing for a bigger building than the one we were in at the time. The people in charge of the Forum deal and the banks and the finance companies didn't understand that their "no" was nothing but a little two-letter word to us. We'd already gone through our Trinity Building experience and had learned how to handle negatives.

We had tried to buy a four-level, 87,000 square foot office building and lost the bid. I was even called a false prophet by some ladies who eventually left our church. They said, "The Lord did not give us that building," and claimed that I was wrong to have pursued it. It took us three years, but the "no" was changed to a "yes" and we got the building.

We had learned that God's delays are not necessarily denials. In spite of the repeated declinations of our loan (close to two dozen institutions turned us down) I knew we only needed one "yes" to cancel out all the "nos." So we just kept knocking on doors and showing our preparedness to people who mattered. Today, we own the Forum.

You cannot go into a situation anticipating success unless you're ready to move when opportunity arrives.

Lysippos, the Greek sculptor of ancient times, once fashioned a bronze statue of a man running with his legs and muscles flexed. The runner was baldheaded except for one lock of hair protruding from the front of his head. The title of the sculpture was *Kairos* (Greek for "opportunity"). The story behind the sculpture was that great opportunities rarely come around. As one approaches, you must snatch it by the hair to get a good grip on it. But if you try to reach for it too late, you will only hit the slick of the bald head, because there's nothing to hold on to. The point of the sculpture is that you may only have one chance to grab opportunity when it comes around, so be ready. Readiness takes preparation. And preparation takes discipline.

CHAMPIONS GET DISCIPLINED

"Only be strong and very courageous; be careful to do according to all the law which Moses My servant commanded you; do not turn from it to the right or to the left, so that you may have success wherever you go" (Joshua 1:7 NASB, emphasis added).

Joshua 1:7 warns us not to turn from God's laws. The idea is to keep your attention on what God has said, and remain focused. Once you determine what God is calling you to do, become single-minded in your pursuit of it.

It's amazing how many people let things get them off course. Sometimes discouragement can throw them off. Sometimes negativity and opposition can lead them astray. But the Word says, "Don't turn to the right or to the left." In many cases, "turning" can suggest taking a detour or seeking a shortcut. Don't yield to that temptation. Steady your course and live a life of discipline. It is no accident that we are called to be disciples and that the word *disciple* is related to the word *discipline*. Many people want to be disciples but don't want to be disciplined people. In order to be a champion, you must get disciplined. You must not let discouragement turn you to the right or to the left. You must not let others turn you away from God's Word or from His direction and purpose for you. God's Word, God's will, and God's way ought to be your priority.

People who you allow to speak into your life—whose words and opinions you value and follow and whose influences hold sway over you—and factors that would influence you to turn to the right or to the left of your course are important building blocks of integrity and character in the life of a champion. Champions are willing to let God lead them and are not turned away from Him by others. You cannot remain within the will of God and seek success by any other means than His. As a believer, you have no other option.

Abram (before God changed his name to Abraham in Genesis 17) allowed himself to be turned. Abram had a God-given destiny. When Abram was 90 years old, the Lord told him He was going to give him and Sarai (before God changed her name to Sarah, also in Genesis 17) a son (see Gen. 17). Sarai laughed with skepticism when she heard the news, because she wasn't much younger than Abram. And then, after several years and no pregnancy, in desperation and in weakness, Abram allowed his wife to convince him to turn from God's path...

> *Now Sarai, Abram's wife, had borne him no children. And she had an Egyptian maidservant whose name was Hagar. So Sarai said to Abram, "See now, the Lord has restrained me from bearing children. Please, go in to my maid; perhaps I shall obtain children by her." And Abram heeded the voice of Sarai. Then Sarai, Abram's wife, took Hagar her maid, the Egyptian, and gave her to her husband Abram to be his wife, after Abram had dwelt ten years in the land of Canaan* (Genesis 16:1-3 NKJV).

A champion knows when to say "no." That may be one of the greatest and most difficult lessons each of us must learn. *No* is one of the most powerful words in the English language, yet we don't use it nearly enough. Champions cannot allow themselves such a fragile ego, or to be so emotionally needy, that they cannot handle turning someone down. It is fear of rejection by humanity that causes people to say "yes" when they know that's the wrong answer. In effect, when you agree to something you should not agree to, you are saying you disagree with God.

Champions do not live undisciplined lives. Lack of discipline leads to compromise. When you compromise, you are asking God to bless what He has not ordained. For example, a Christian businessman might be working hard at the office all week long, asking God for wisdom, direction, and guidance to assist him in his daily decisions. But if he lives with his girlfriend, then his personal life lacks godly discipline. A life of hypocrisy and compromise, of picking and choosing which of God's commands to follow or not, is nothing more than disobedience. According to God's standards, that person is ill-prepared to be a true champion.

A champion's success is tied directly to obedience to God. As you seek to become a champion, then you must be prepared to walk in God's ways as a habit of life.

Be strong, show yourself a man, and observe what the Lord your God requires: Walk in His ways, and keep His decrees and commands, His laws and requirements, as written in the Law of Moses, so that you may prosper in all you do and wherever you go (1 Kings 2:2-3 NIV).

The word *observe* is an outflow of the concept of *study*. In other words, in order for us to do what God requires us to do, we must first know what God has said. To know what He has said can only be accomplished as we spend time in His Word. Spending time in the Word, being prepared to move from one season to the next, sitting under the tutelage of a mentor, being ready when opportunity arises, and learning self-discipline prepares champions to handle successfully all that life can ever throw at them.

"Champions do not become champions when they win the event, but in the hours, weeks, months, and years they spend preparing for it. The victorious performance itself is merely the demonstration of their championship character."

—T. Alan Armstrong

ENDNOTES

1. Spencer Johnson, M.D., *Who Moved My Cheese?* (New York, NY: G.P. Putnam's Sons, 1998).

2. The great prophet Elijah also had his own way of parting the Jordan river: Second Kings 2:8 tells how he rolled up his cloak and struck the water with it and the river divided, allowing him and Elisha to cross over on dry ground.

3. Moses was strong and vigorous when he died, despite being 120 years old. Deuteronomy 34:7 states that when Moses died, "his eyes were not dim nor his natural vigor diminished" (Deut. 34:7 NKJV). Thus, the changing of the guard had nothing to do with age or health or diminished capacity. Rather, it came about as a result of Moses disobeying God in striking the rock (see Num. 20:11-12), thus causing him to

lose out on the privilege of leading the Israelites across the Jordan River and into the Promised Land.

4. While that lack of preparation could be blamed on the evils of apartheid (just as slavery in America for 300 years halted civil rights and opportunities for Americans of African descent), still there were no leaders in South Africa who had the foresight necessary to prepare that current and next generation during apartheid, so that they could step up if or when apartheid were to end—which, of course, it did.

Chapter 4

The Breakfast of Champions

BABE Ruth, Michael Jordan, Althea Gibson, and Jesse Owens have in common that they are among a unique fraternity of athletes who have appeared on the Wheaties breakfast cereal box.

Since 1934 when the first athlete, baseball great Lou Gehrig, was featured on the front of a Wheaties package, young boys and girls across the nation have grown up with an aspiration to see their own name and face on the iconic orange box. Wheaties is much more than a mere breakfast cereal. It's an American icon. The famous box is recognizable with or without the name. More than anything else, it is known for its slogan: *Breakfast of Champions*. For more than a quarter of a century now, that motto can be paraphrased into the call of God on my own life, summarized, as I mentioned in the introduction, by these five words: **Building Champions for Divine Deployment.**

To build a champion—a woman or man of God—you begin with a good, solid diet of the Word of God. There are times when God's Word might taste a little bitter, but if you will trust God and take His Word into you, it will always have the desired effect: to build you into a champion.

An Unlikely Champion

The example that the prophet Jeremiah set more than six hundred years before Christ was born still stands as spiritual nourishment for champions today. And yet, Jeremiah was an unlikely candidate for championship (he was probably the last person you'd ever picture on a Wheaties box!). But sometimes, true champions are not immediately obvious.

Jeremiah was born in the village of Anathoth. He was a contemporary of the prophets Nahum and Habakkuk. The great prophet Ezekiel, who was younger than Jeremiah, prophesied in Babylon around the same time that Jeremiah prophesied in Jerusalem.

God commanded Jeremiah not to marry or have children, as an illustration of his message that God's pending judgment hovered over Israel and that the next generation was doomed to destruction.

Jeremiah is known primarily for three things:

1. Jeremiah was uniquely called by God —even before he was born.

Before I formed thee in the belly I knew thee; and before thou camest forth out of the womb I sanctified thee, and I ordained thee a prophet unto the nations (Jeremiah 1:5).

Jeremiah was just as human as the next person. He dealt with personal inward struggles pertaining to his youth, his inadequacies, and his inabilities. He focused on what he could not do, and on areas in which he felt weak or ill-equipped. In fact, when God called him, you could say that, in today's colloquialism, Jeremiah basically responded, "Ah, Lord God! C'mon—I can't do that! Look at me—I'm way too young. I can't even speak well!" (see Jer. 1:6). He felt he was just a kid and was afraid people wouldn't take him seriously.

But God told him not to worry about all that, and not to be afraid; He would put His words in Jeremiah's mouth and everything would be fine (see Jer. 1:7-8). And Jeremiah of Anathoth went on to become a major prophet, listed right up there with Isaiah, Ezekiel, and Daniel.

> *Then said I: "Ah, Lord God! Behold, I cannot speak, for I am a youth." But the Lord said to me: "Do not say, 'I am a youth,' for you shall go to all to whom I send you, and whatever I command you, you shall speak. Do not be afraid of their faces, for I am with you to deliver you," says the Lord* (Jeremiah 1:6-8 NKJV).

2. JEREMIAH WAS KNOWN AS "THE WEEPING PROPHET."

Jeremiah is known as the weeping prophet because he openly wept over the sins of the people in his grief over how far Israel had strayed from God. (See Jeremiah 9.)

Have you ever shed tears over sins you committed that hurt not only you but others? I would venture a guess that many Christians have never been so broken by what they had done that they actually wept. Fewer still have probably cried openly at the unrighteousness swirling around the world today. With what is happening in our nation, there wouldn't have been enough tears for Jeremiah to shed today. He cried over the blatant sins that were being carried on in the very face of God. He was a picture of Jesus, who cried over the city of Jerusalem (see Luke 19:41).

3. JEREMIAH OFTEN BECAME DISCOURAGED.

The third thing Jeremiah is known for is that he got discouraged. He became disheartened at what seemed like a lack of progress in his ministry, the Israelites' determination to disobey Jehovah, and the intense persecution hurled at him as a prophet of God. Things got so bad that Jeremiah even tried to go on strike...

I will not make mention of Him [God], *nor speak anymore in His name* (Jeremiah 20:9).

The great prophet basically told God, "Alright, if that's the way it's going to be, I'll just shut up. I'm not speaking anymore. I'm not going to temple anymore. I'm not going to prophesy anymore. I'm not going to pray anymore. I'm not going to minister anymore. I'm not going to be used of You anymore. I'm outta here. I quit. Good-bye."

Jeremiah decided to throw in the towel because of all the complacency and outright disobedience and evil going on. He was broken, hurt, and discouraged by the degeneration of society.

We've all had times when we have become so disheartened that we thought about giving up. Sometimes we think life would be easier if we just pack it in and give it up. I've thought about giving up before, actually I thought about it many times (often on Sunday nights). At times, it seemed as though that was the only peaceful solution to the constant pressures and struggles I was facing. No matter what I tried to do, nothing seemed to go right. There were moments when it looked like the only way relief would come would be if I just surrendered and threw in the towel and cried out, "Enough!"

The Scripture paints a great picture: the mighty prophet Jeremiah giving himself his own little pity party as he struggled with God and told Him, "I'll never speak again!" He even went so far as to blame everything on God:

> *O Lord, you deceived me, and I was deceived; you overpowered me and prevailed. I am ridiculed all day long; everyone mocks me. Whenever I speak, I cry out proclaiming violence and destruction. So the word of the Lord has brought me insult and reproach all day long* (Jeremiah 20:7-9 NIV).

But as he lamented before God, something began to burn deep down inside his spirit, and the champion in this great man of God would not allow him to accept defeat. For, after he mouthed these words—after he proclaimed that he'd never worship again, never praise again, never minister again—at the moment he decided to remain silent concerning the things of God, something began to move within him:

But His word was in my heart like a burning fire shut up in my bones; I was weary of holding it back, and I could not (Jeremiah 20:9b NKJV).

What an incredible self-realization. Jeremiah said he wanted to quit, but he could not, because the word that God had placed in him was *like fire shut up in his bones.* Such a powerful, compelling push, an overwhelming drive of God, was placed in Jeremiah's spirit that he simply could not ignore it. He could no more walk away from his calling than he could walk away from breathing. *What You have placed within me must come out!*

What God has placed in you must come out, too. When God places a word, a call, a vision inside you, *it must come out*—it's like a roaring fire shut up inside of you.

THE RIGHT DIET

Jeremiah fed on the diet of champions...

Your words were found, and I ate them, and Your word was to me the joy and rejoicing of my heart; for I am called by Your name, O Lord God of hosts (Jeremiah 15:16 NKJV).

The passage above unfolds into four sections:

1. **I found Your Word.**

2. I ate Your Word.

3. I was blessed by Your Word.

4. I am covered by Your Word.

Let's examine them each...

1: "I FOUND YOUR WORD"

This is a phrase that indicates that the person had been on a search. The word *found* is used in the same context as in the parable of the man digging for treasure, or the person searching for the pearl of great price, or the missing coin. It's the same concept as the shepherd going after a lost sheep. It speaks of intent to seek, and the result of the search. "I've *found* what I was looking for!" The text does not imply an accidental discovery. It indicates one who is searching diligently and deliberately with a desire to find and to experience that which he seeks. "I found it," means, "I found it *because I searched for it.*"

The idea of *found* also has to do with enlightenment. When you *find* God's Word, it means that you have realized the true *essence* of it. It's like saying that the Bible is no longer a book filled with words; it's suddenly a *revelation*. Its meaning has become evident. It's no longer hidden. Like a light turned on in a dark room, the truth of the Scriptures is seen for what it is, and no matter how many times you may have heard it before, this time you *get* it. This is because words are no more than the verbal expression, codification, and organization of thoughts; whereas the revelation of the *intent* of the message the words reveal is what gives that *Ah-ha!* moment when we suddenly get it. No matter how many times you've read the message before, this time it hits you.

"Your words were found," suggests that, in so finding, Jeremiah discovered something about *the way God thinks*. God wanted the prophet to understand something about this quest he was on. In Jeremiah's search for God's Word, it was important that he recognize that God's thoughts were not his thoughts (see Isa. 55:8-9). God's plans were not Jeremiah's plans.

God doesn't do things the way you and I do them. In other words, there is an ever-present dimension of the unknowable in the thoughts and the ways of God. Thus, in order to find the Word of God, one must find, realize, and receive the mind of God and the thoughts He has chosen to make available to us. We cannot know God's thoughts on our own. God is saying, "You can't figure Me out. That which you know about Me is only because I disclosed it to you. And one of the ways I disclose Myself is through My Word." The revelation is simply to receive what God has chosen to release. When Jeremiah said he found God's Word, it meant that he gained some insight into God's thoughts. Likewise, when we "find" the Word of God, we have just been given revelation of the mind of God, His thoughts, His purpose, so that we now have a greater understanding of who He is *and* who we are *in Him*.

One time way back when I was in high school, a woman called my mother and told her somebody saw me doing something I should not have done. Although I had actually *not* done what I was accused of, this lady called my momma and said, "Ruth, let me tell you what that boy did." And she proceeded to give a detailed accusation against me.

Momma listened, and then she responded, "No. He did not do that. Now, he may have done something else, but he did not do that." This was because my momma knew me well enough to know how I think, how I talk, how I behave. The woman had said I had done something specific in a certain way. Momma said, "Oh no, he didn't do that." She knew I would never talk that way to an adult. My mother knew my ways and my words. Therefore, her knowledge of me as a person and as her son existed before this woman accused me.

"I have found your Word" implies that it was there before Jeremiah found it. It does not mean that the revelation brought by the word began *when* he found it; it *was there before he found it*. The point is this: in John 1:1 and 1:14, when the apostle said, "In the beginning was the Word, and the Word was with God, and the Word was God. ...and the Word was made flesh, and dwelt among us," he was implying metaphorically and spiritually that the physical manifestation of the revelation of God's Word *is Jesus Christ*.

Now, this might be a hermeneutical, interpretative stretch, but just for the sake of discussion, let's relate John's revelation to Jeremiah's statement—and its eye-opening conclusion:

"In the beginning was the Word" = The Word that Jeremiah found existed before he found it

"The Word was made flesh" = Jesus the Christ (who was there in the beginning and *is* the Word)

The Word Jeremiah found = Jesus

Conclusion = Jeremiah found Jesus

When Jeremiah said, "Your Words were found," he was saying that he received the spiritual revelation and physiological manifestation of God's Word: Jesus Christ—even though Jeremiah couldn't put a specific name to Him other than Jehovah, since the physical incarnation of God born as man had not yet taken place.

Back in the seventies, Bill Bright, former leader of Campus Crusade for Christ, launched a brilliant national campaign with a simple slogan: *I Found It*. He had the whole nation buzzing for months over those three little words. He spent millions of dollars plastering "I Found It" on billboards across America. People from all walks of life wanted to know what the "it" was that had been found. Then, after months of this mysterious "advertising," Mr. Bright mobilized thousands of young people to evangelize door-to-door all across the nation, beginning with the statement, "I found it." What those young students had found was the fact that Jesus is the Christ, and they went out to tell the world. The result of that ingenious campaign was that thousands of people came to know Christ because somebody had simply told them what they had found.

Look again at the words of Jeremiah. Notice that he didn't say he found religion or spirituality or a deeper meaning to life. He didn't say he found Jehovah. He didn't say he found the local temple. Didn't say he found religion. He said he found God's Word.

Then, after Jeremiah found God's Word, he said he did something very peculiar…

2: "I ATE YOUR WORD"

On her way to college one day, one of my goddaughters wrote to me and asked, "When you're reading Scripture, do you take every word literally?"

I shared with her a fundamental biblical principle that I had learned back when I was in school: *begin with the literal when the literal makes sense.* Assume that what the text of the Word of God says is literally what the writer meant, as long as it makes literal sense.

If this is the case, then what is the meaning of the Jeremiah 15:16 passage, "Your words were found, and I ate them?" For some, the Bible seems to contain a bit too much roughage for their diet. First of all, to say that Jeremiah "ate" God's Word means that he ingested it. In other words, he received the Word literally into his being. He didn't say, "I found it and I read it," nor, "I found it, memorized it, and quoted it." No; what he did was to take the living Word of God and receive it into his life so deeply that it became dispersed throughout the very core and essence of his being—so much so that every part of his body was affected by what he ate. It became a revelation of who he was—of his thoughts and his personhood—in God.

Eating God's Word is a whole level of commitment that challenges every person who wants to be a champion. It speaks of total ingestion: you receive the Word of God into you in order to impact and affect every area of your life. The text implies that Jeremiah *ate it as a meal.* Thus, God's Word is the quintessential breakfast of the real champion.

SPIRITUAL MALNOURISHMENT

Hunger is one of the global tragedies of our time. Millions of people in third world countries go to sleep without food. However, probably the people you know eat every day—most eat three times per day. If you only eat once per week, you will no doubt eventually suffer from severe malnourishment. Likewise, if you eat of God's Word only one meal per week, you will wither from lack of spiritual nourishment. Unfortunately in our culture, most believers partake of spiritual food only one time per week, usually during a church service (where many Christians have to be spoon-fed like babies). They might snack during the week on a cute little memory verse here and there, but they go around as spiritual skeletons.

There is an affliction of spiritual anorexia coursing throughout the church today. We've become a nation of biblical anemics. People only want just enough of God's Word to squeak by. Nowadays, in our politically correct society, the only spiritual food that a growing number of people can tolerate is a bland serving of "bibliopablum" (I made up that word) that downplays the name of Jesus, doesn't dare mention obedience, puts little emphasis on the power of real prayer, stays away from discussion of a literal hell, and prohibits coming out against certain hot-button issues, because heaven forbid some poor soul in the pew should become offended if the pastor serves up too much biblical protein.

Let me be real clear: if you sit under biblical teaching that rarely offends, then you are not being taught the full and complete Gospel—the one that builds champions. In order to be a true champion, you must have a steady spiritual diet that promotes growth in your inner being. And that means roughage. That means protein. That means grit: The Wonder Bread of Life; The Breakfast of Champions; The Word of the Almighty Living God.

THE BREAD OF LIFE

In John 6:48, Jesus said, "I am the bread of life" (John 6:48 NKJV). Just as you need daily bread physically, you also need daily bread spiritually, because spiritual bread is the enhancement of your personal relationship with Jesus Christ. When Jesus broke bread during the Last Supper and said, "Take, eat: this is my body" (Mark 14:22), He was speaking not only of His essence as the Christ, but also of His power, which we need on a daily basis. You cannot make it without it.

Champions dare not even attempt life without having eaten His daily bread. They don't even try to be what God has called them to be without being empowered by the nutrients and blessings and vitamins and proteins that He provides by His presence and power and Word.

The devil is out to do all he can to starve you of God's presence and power, because when you're spiritually malnourished, when you don't eat of God's Word, you become a prime target for the enemy—who rarely attacks us when we're strong, but mostly at our weak points. Satan uses the same strategy that nature employs. In a fight for the survival of the fittest, a lion will study a herd of antelope to determine its weakest member, then isolate that member, attack it, and take it down.

When Israel was attacked by the Amalikites, their enemy had an interesting battle strategy. They attacked from the rear where the Israelites were weary and weak. The Bible says they attacked the "stragglers" (see Deut. 25:17-18 NKJV). Those who were distanced from the rest of God's people were easy prey for the enemy. Your spiritual strength is drained when you are not being nourished by the Bread of life. You become an easy target for the devil.

The devil, who walks about like a roaring lion, seeking whom he may devour (see 1 Pet. 5:8), does the same thing: he cunningly and patiently lures you away from the meat of the study of the

Word of God, eases you away from fellowship in the Body so you spend less and less quality time with your brothers and sisters in Christ, then attacks you where you are most vulnerable, and takes you down.

Many Christians appear to be healthy and look good and well nourished on Sunday mornings, praising the Lord to the high rafters during church service. But by the time Monday or Tuesday roll around (and in some cases even Sunday night), they're weak as mice, and satan swoops in for an easy snack.

The Word isn't simply window dressing. It's your minimum daily requirement of the essential nutrients needed to build healthy champions. It is what Jesus identified as the fuel that fired His entire earthly life:

Jesus said to them, "My food is to do the will of Him who sent Me, and to finish His work" (John 4:34 NKJV).

3: "I Was Blessed by Your Word"

After Jeremiah ate God's Words, he said, "they were my joy and my heart's delight" (Jer. 15:16 NIV). In the same way that natural food metabolizes into physical energy, God does something when we take His Word into our spirit, into our life, into the essence of our being on a daily basis in relationship with Him: it produces joy and rejoicing deep down inside of us.

Attitude is fueled by faith. *Joy* is primarily an attitude word, because it impacts the way we see life. If you view life through the lens of joy, then you will respond with an attitude of joy. Joy always looks two ways: in the *now*, and in the now *relative to the not yet.* One of the joys of God's Word is that it lets you know that where you are is not necessarily where you will stay. You're on your way up from where you are; and that should add to your joy.

Joy is a continual state of mind that is present in spite of circumstances. However, don't confuse joy with happiness, because happiness is based on *happenings.* If you don't possess the joy of the Lord within you, then you are susceptible to being negatively swayed by whatever is happening in your life. No matter what is going on around you, you need something to sustain you within if what is *happening* is not good. The joy of the Word of the Lord is that it is a continuous flow from the limitless wellspring of the Holy Spirit.

When the storms of life are raging, joy is what takes you from the right now into the soon-to-come, because the Word doesn't stop at joy alone, but at joy *and rejoicing* (see Jer. 15:16). You can't have rejoicing until you first get joy, which, according to Galatians 5:22, is one of the fruits, the byproducts, of the Spirit. Thus, one of the things that the Holy Ghost produces in godly champions is joy. Joy is what champions feel in spite of what they see. Joy is the level ground that moves them from now into pretty soon. Joy is what happens along the way.

Joy is continuous; rejoice is spontaneous. Joy is like a watch: it keeps on ticking no matter what's happening in the world. Rain pelting down, the clock is still ticking. Disaster in the world, wars and rumors of wars on every side, but the clock keeps on ticking. Joy can take a licking and keep on ticking, because joy is not affected by what's on the outside; it is sustained by what's on the inside. So every now and then, because I've got joy, my joy over-flows and my joy begins to rejoice.

If joy is like a clock, then *rejoice* is like the alarm on the clock: when the alarm is set, anytime the clock is ticking, the alarm is subject to go off without advance warning. Time keeps ticking and joy goes on and on, but because my clock has an alarm on it, rejoicing can suddenly erupt.

You may be struggling with a challenge in your life, but I'm here to assure you, if you hold on to the Word of God, the alarm is set. God has already programmed it. It's in His computer. Get ready to get up. The rejoice alert of God is about to sound. It does not matter what you're going through, God has set the alarm. When the alarm goes off, it's not time for joy (that goes on all the time when you dine regularly on the food of champions), it's time for *re*joy. It's time to celebrate. It's time to bless His name.

Rejoicing can break out at any moment of any day. As you drive to work, as you shuffle across the parking lot, as you relax during your lunchtime break, as you sit at home with your family at dinnertime. *Rejoice!*

It can happen as you begin to think about working on a job that you think you're not qualified for but God gave you a shot at. *Rejoice!*

When you think about "Who" got you that promotion—*rejoice!*

How He made a way out of no way—*rejoice!*

The more you think, the more you thank Him, and you feel something rising up in you. It's *rejoicing!*

Rejoice in the name of Jesus.

Rejoice for what God has already done.

Rejoice for what God is already doing.

Rejoice for what He's going to do tomorrow.

When I think about the goodness of Jesus and all He has done for me, my spirit cries out, "Hallelujah!" My heart cries out, "Thank You, Jesus!" My mouth cries out, "Bless Your holy name!"

Champions rejoice until they get their deliverance.

Champions rejoice until they get their breakthrough.

Champions rejoice until they get that new job.

Champions rejoice until they get that promotion.

Champions rejoice until they get that raise.

So rejoice!

*Let all those who seek You **rejoice** and be glad in You; and let those who love Your salvation say continually, "Let God be magnified!"* (Psalm 70:4 NKJV)

*This is the day which the Lord hath made; we will **rejoice** and be glad in it* (Psalm 118:24).

*Rejoice in the Lord always: and again I say, **Rejoice*** (Philippians 4:4).

Rejoice evermore (1 Thessalonians. 5:16).

And I could quote on and on, because *rejoice* occurs more than *two hundred times* in the Bible.

REJOICE: IT'S A CHOICE

Champions understand that rejoicing *is a decision that one makes*. You can *choose* to rejoice. You rejoice out of the joy that is the fruit and result of the presence of the living God in your life. It does not mean that every day is sunshine and roses. It does not mean that you have no problems and no challenges. Jeremiah was a man who had faced a life of discouragement. And yet, because he ate the Word of God as an act of his will and as an overflow of his joy, he rejoiced in the God of his salvation.

The prophets spoke of the sound of joy (see Ezek. 7:7; Isa. 12:3; Jer. 48:33). Joy is more than a mere state of inner condition; it is to be *expressed*. The Bible pictures it as a shout, a cheer, a blast of sound as with a trumpet, a war cry, the sound of an alarm, a shout of victory, and even an applause. Sometimes joy is expressed by weeping. There are almost 30 words used in the Old Testament alone that speak of joy or rejoicing. The bottom line is that in all of the pictures painted by the words for joy and rejoicing, all of them imply an uncontainable outward expression of an inner state of well-being. It is more an expression than an emotion. When the inner emotion is expressed, joy becomes rejoicing. It is hard to be cool and sophisticated when you rejoice. It is hard to be reserved and elegant when you rejoice.

Jeremiah says the word of the Lord was both joy and rejoicing. He received it and it produced joy, and then he released it as rejoicing. No wonder Paul says in Philippians 4:4, "Rejoice…and again I say rejoice." It's as if Paul is saying, "I'm not playing now—you guys better rejoice!"

So far, we've examined the progress of Jeremiah's praise to God, from:

"Your words were found" =

The revelation of God's thoughts and His Person

to:

"I ate them" =

Intimacy of relationship with God disbursed throughout the very essence and fiber of my being and my body

to:

"Your word was to me

the joy and rejoicing of my heart" =

It produced joy within me and rejoicing from me

And finally, to the summation of Jeremiah's praise:

4: "I Am Covered by Your Word"

The closing words of Jeremiah's discourse bestow upon the champion perhaps the greatest covering of all: you are called by His name, "Lord of Hosts" (see Jer. 15:16).

Lord of Hosts is a military term that speaks of God as the Commander of armies (or "resources"), which He releases into your life that you might become all He has ordained and called you to be. In other words, you are covered by your Commander; He "backs your play." Day by day, the resources that are under the control of the very Creator of the universe—a God who is committed to making you a champion—are made available to you. Since He has ordained that nothing can separate you from Him, He has your back. In relationships, in finances, in the boardroom, in family challenges, in every problem that you face, God is in your corner. I pray you will get that truth into your spirit.

Whenever you are ready to eat and be nourished, on the menu is the Main Course, the Appetizer, the Dessert, the Bread of Life, the All-in-All, the ultimate Breakfast of Champions, rolled into one meal: Jesus Christ. Eat of Him, and you will *never* hunger.

Jesus said unto them, I am the bread of life: he that cometh to me shall never hunger; and he that believeth on me shall never thirst (John 6:35).

Chapter 5

The Trials of a Champion

*What then shall we say to these things? If God is for us, who can
be against us? He who did not spare His own Son, but delivered
Him up for us all, how shall He not with Him also freely give
us all things? Who shall bring a charge against God's elect? It is
God who justifies. Who is he who condemns? It is Christ who
died, and furthermore is also risen, who is even at the right
hand of God, who also makes intercession for us. Who shall separate us from the love of Christ? Shall tribulation, or distress, or
persecution, or famine, or nakedness, or peril, or sword? As it is
written: "For Your sake we are killed all day long; we are
accounted as sheep for the slaughter." Yet in all these things we
are more than conquerors through Him who loved us* (Romans
8:31-37 NKJV).

To overcome the endless trials of life, champions must first
train their minds to think like champions.

Paul begins the passage with the question, "What then shall we say to these things?" and he concludes with the answer, "In all these things we are more than conquerors" (see Rom. 8:31-37 NKJV). Notice the connection. Paul is saying in verse 31 that we need to respond to the things he covered throughout his Romans 8 discourse,[1] the message of which is that when we are in Jesus, we have been freed from banishment from God (which otherwise would have been our due punishment because of indwelling sin). In other words, Paul is assuring us that when we are living our lives under grace of the salvation of the Lord and are walking according to the Spirit and not according to the enticements of the world, then not only are we not condemned, but as "more than conquerors," we are *champions*.

Thus, the first step in your walk as more than a conqueror, the most urgent beginning concept for you to grasp during your trials as a Christian, is to get into your spirit that *you are **already** a champion*. God does not condemn you. God is not out to get you. God is not holding you prisoner to your past. God is not angry with you. Paul makes that pretty clear when he says in Romans 8:1 that there is now no condemnation. He hammers that point home by adding, in verses 14 through 16, that if we allow ourselves to be led by the Spirit of God, then we are children of God—a fact to which the Holy Spirit Himself bears witness:

> *Those who are led by the Spirit of God are sons of God.... The Spirit himself testifies with our spirit that we are God's children. Now if we are children, then we are heirs—heirs of God and co-heirs with Christ, if indeed we share in His sufferings in order that we may also share in His glory* (Romans 8:14, 16-17 NIV).

CALLED ACCORDING TO HIS PURPOSE

*For whom He foreknew, He also predestined to be conformed to
the image of His Son, that He might be the firstborn among
many brethren. Moreover whom He predestined, these He also
called; whom He called, these He also justified; and whom He
justified, these He also glorified* (Romans 8:29-30 NKJV).

With the foundation of our identity laid in Romans 8:14 and
16-17, Paul then goes on, in Romans 8:28, to tell us that God has
called us according to His purpose, which means that we are not
here by accident (see Rom. 8:14,16-17,28). It does not matter the
circumstances under which you were born, your being here is not
some unexpected occurrence. You were not just made and then
tossed to Earth to fend for yourself for seventy or eighty years. Your
life is not a fluke. You are not mere happenstance. God doesn't
work that way. God has a plan, and you are part of His purpose.
You have been called out of your past (and the sins thereof) and
into your future, which has a purpose. And you are to live your life
fulfilling that purpose.

Paul nails that point down by stating in Romans 8:30 that not
only were we called according to God's purpose, but that we were
predestined to be glorified (see Rom. 8:30). Now I don't want to get
caught up in doctrinal wrangling, but it is important to understand
that the biblical concept of *predestination* means "to mark off or set
up boundaries and limits beforehand."[2] The idea of Paul's revelation is that you have lived your life within the preset boundaries of
God, and the road of your life led you to the saving grace and love

of God. The journey of your life has led you to salvation, *not* condemnation (see Rom. 8:1).[4]

What an incredible, crucial, powerful revelation on your journey as a champion: the gold medal has been *set aside for you.* It is important that you get that into your spirit. All you have to do is follow the road that leads to that victory. And God clearly identifies the road to follow: Jesus. You do have a choice—you don't *have* to choose God's road and go and collect your win. But it's there, set aside for you for the taking at the end of that road.

Everything in Romans 8:29-30 is a journey. It speaks of God's foreknowledge of every aspect of our life and explains that the destiny to which God has called us on our journey is a destiny of glory. We have been called to glorify God. Our purpose is to live our life to His glory. The will and purpose of God is that we glorify Him and that we be glorified before Him. And He prepares us well for the trials we will face upon our journey during life.

Romans 8:28-30 enumerates three foundational truths for the Christian:

1. **You are no longer condemned.**

2. **Your life in Christ was predestined.**

3. **You now have an important purpose to fulfill.**

Then, in Romans 8:31, Paul sums it all up with one crucial question: "What shall we then say to these things?" The *New International Version* asks it this way: "What, then, shall we say in response to this?" (Rom. 8:31 NIV). *The Living Bible* asks it as, "What can we ever say to such wonderful things as these?" (Rom. 8:31 TLB).

Saved.

Children of God.

No longer condemned.

Filled with the Spirit of God.

In direct relationship with our Creator.

Astounding truths! Your condition was that you were once a sinner condemned to death and eternal separation from God. But your position now is that you are a child of the living God, and His Spirit now dwells in you and gives you confirmation in your spirit that you are a daughter or son of the Most High Almighty God. And because you are a part of the family of God, *you have a purpose.* That is an amazing fact that so many Christians either don't fully grasp or simply gloss over. It should have a great impact on us. The truth that we are in relationship with God should bear directly on our daily behavior, our words, our attitudes, and our actions toward others. The question that continually shadows the champion is this: "Is my life journey making a *difference* in the world, now that I know who I really am?"

After asking what we shall say to the issues he raised throughout Romans 8, Paul then raises four key questions…

FIRST QUESTION: ROMANS 8:31— "IF GOD BE FOR US, WHO CAN BE AGAINST US?"

"If God is with us, who can mess with us?" would be a loose translation in today's vernacular. What shall we say to that? Obviously we would say, "God is for us."

You are a champion, you are an overcomer, you are a conqueror. Why? Because God is for you. This is not some spiritual ego trip. This is not a statement of theological superiority. It is a simple statement of spiritual and theological *fact*. That God is for us is a statement of humility.

Over and over, God has made a commitment to never leave us:

"The Lord your God goes with you; he will never leave you nor forsake you" (Deuteronomy 31:6 NIV).

"He is the One who goes with you. He will not leave you nor forsake you" (Deuteronomy 31:6 NKJV).

I will not fail thee, nor forsake thee (Joshua 1:5).

For the Lord God, even my God, will be with thee; he will not fail thee, nor forsake thee (1 Chronicles 28:20).

God has said, "Never will I leave you; never will I forsake you" (Hebrews 13:5 NIV).

In a related question, designed to buttress God's demonstration of the truth that God is not out to get you and will not abandon you, Paul then asks a rhetorical question:

He that spared not his own Son, but delivered him up for us all, how shall he not with him also freely give us all things? (Romans 8:32)

Paul is making the argument from a point of view of the Greater to the lesser. In other words, since God loves you enough to give you the gift of His only Son, Jesus, that proves He loves you enough to freely give you everything you need to live your life as a champion. Period. It proves that *God is for us.* He has given us everything we need to win—but we have to get in the game and play it His way. Why? Because it is our Father's good pleasure to give us the Kingdom (see Luke 12:32), and every good gift and every perfect gift is from above and comes down from our Father (see James 1:17).

God made a commitment to us all the way. We don't deserve it—*grace* is the very definition of our relationship with Him. But the demonstration of His grace and His mercy is that He is so committed to making you a champion that He gives you everything you need to become one. *Everything!* Nothing is lacking for God's children.

So, if God is on your side, who is it that can stand effectively against you? *Nobody.*

SECOND QUESTION: ROMANS 8:33— "WHO SHALL LAY ANY THING TO THE CHARGE OF GOD'S ELECT?"

The Living Bible puts it this way: "Who dares accuse us whom God has chosen for His own?" (see Rom. 8:33 TLB). Paul, in essence, stands before the universe and says, "Is there anybody out there who can make a charge stick against God's elect?" In reality, it's a loaded question. The answer is that no one can make a charge stick against you. But there's a revelation in the test: He is asking who can bring an accusation *and make it stick*.

It's like the question ministers used to ask in wedding ceremonies just before they made their pronouncement of marriage: "Is there anybody here who knows of any reason why this man and this woman should not be joined in holy matrimony?" Everybody holds their breath for a moment, but usually nobody ever steps forward to bring a charge, because the question is more of a formality than an attempt to initiate a serious inquest (although I do know of a few instances where some crazy stuff happened at that question!).

However, notice that Paul's question and its ancillary follow-up are in the form of a legal inquiry, which could be read as: "Who can lay a charge against God's elect *and make it stick*—especially since it is God alone who justifies His own?" The key phrase is "...against God's elect." The word *elect* means "already chosen." Remember, it is God who justifies. So here's the inquiry in layman's terms: since you are God's and He has declared you to be without condemnation, and He alone is the Judge anyway, who can go into a court and file a criminal charge against you and make the charge stick and get you locked up? *Nobody* can bring a charge before God and make it stick against someone God has already chosen and declared not condemned.

God has already judged you, and you have been justified. The word *justify* is a term indicating that a person has been acquitted of all charges and declared righteous and innocent. Here's the catch:

John 8:44 says the devil is a liar and the father of all lies—but when he comes before God, the devil doesn't lie about you; he *accuses* you (see John 8:44). The Bible calls the devil *the accuser of the brethren* (see Rev. 12:10). Jesus says of satan, "When he lies, he speaks his native language, for he is a liar and the father of lies" (John 8:44 NIV).

Clearly, the devil is a liar and a deceiver. But when he goes whining to God to accuse you of something, he doesn't have to lie, because the enemy's tactic is to point out what you *did* do. You know you did it. God knows you did it. The devil knows you did it. But where the devil always goofs up is that when he runs to the court of God to file charges against you, by the time he arrives, the case is already over because God has already declared you righteous. You were acquitted before ol' Beelzebub trotted in to file his charges. Case closed.

Being acquitted doesn't mean you didn't do it; it just means you've been found not guilty and don't have to pay a penalty. The court is satisfied. The devil doesn't have to make stuff up. He simply files a complaint with God about what you did, which means that, yes, you did it, no contest there, but every time the accuser shows up to try to file a charge against you, Jesus tells the court you've been pardoned. And every time the devil tries to bring a new charge against you, Jesus raises His hand and says to God, "Your Honor, I'm here to represent the accused. The penalty for that crime has already been paid." Next case.

These incessant proceedings probably get so tiresome that after awhile, instead of Jesus saying a word, all He does is just raise a hand, and on that hand, Judge God can see scars from the nails.

Then Judge God slams down the gavel and states, "Penalty paid. Defendant is released."

One of the problems with a minister asking the question, "Is there anyone here who knows of any reason why these two should not be joined in holy matrimony?" is that by then it's too late, because by the time a couple gets to the altar, the final decision has already been made. Paul says the same thing: by the time the enemy comes to lay a charge against you, the case has already been adjudicated, decided, and closed. No punishment shall be passed out. You have been declared righteous.

Nothing but the grace of the living God is able to look beyond our faults. And "if we confess our sins, he is faithful and just to forgive us our sins, and to cleanse us from all unrighteousness" (1 John 1:9) and look at us as though we never did it in the first place. The nail-scarred hands of Jesus rise up and He says, "I paid for that one—and I still chose her. I know what he did, and I still chose him." That level of unconditional love is what makes the champion *want* to live life God's way.

So who is it that can lay a charge against you and make it stick? *Nobody.*

THIRD QUESTION: ROMANS 8:34—"WHO IS HE WHO CONDEMNS?" (NKJV)

Back to the courtroom. It's a rigged trial. This case is fixed. Jury tampering found its way into the proceedings way back before the foundation of the world. *Who can condemn us?* Watch the revelation of the text that follows the question:

It is Christ who died, and furthermore is also risen, who is even at the right hand of God, who also makes intercession for us (Romans 8:34 NKJV).

The only person who has the right to judge you and condemn you is the One who died for you—which means you cannot allow yourself to lose sleep at night worrying about what people think about you. Nobody can judge you outside of the One who made you, and He's on *your* side. I don't say that arrogantly. I say that because of your condition in Christ: He has already shown that He is with you by dying for you and rising again and maintaining His position interceding for you at the right hand of God.

It's as if when your case comes before the Judge, you don't even need to show up with an attorney. Because Jesus, as the District Attorney charged with prosecuting cases against the accused, turns to the Judge and says, "The State is dropping this particular case, Your Honor." Boom—charges dropped, case over.

The reason you are a champion is because you have Someone in that courtroom interceding for you and preventing anyone from bringing a charge against you.

And now to the final (and perhaps most important) question asked by Paul in his summation of Romans 8…

FOURTH QUESTION: ROMANS 8:35—"WHO SHALL SEPARATE US FROM THE LOVE OF CHRIST?"

The word *separate* in the passage above carries with it the idea of "bringing space between" or "removing apart from." It symbolizes a pulling away from the embrace of God. This is another rhetorical question, which obviously infers a negative answer: no one can separate us from the love of Jesus.

The love of God holds you so tightly that no devil in hell can pry you away from the loving embrace of God. There's nothing even *you* can do to make God stop loving you. Let that incredible truth simmer down into your spirit for a moment—it is important for the champion to grasp that profound fact. There's nothing you have ever done that can make God stop loving you. There is nothing you can ever do to make Him stop loving you. Think about that. What can separate you, remove you, pull you out of the loving embrace of God? *Nothing.* I don't care what you did. I don't care what happened to you. There's nothing that life could ever throw at you that could rip you from the grasp of God's love.[4] Ask the thief on the Cross, from Luke 23:43. Ask former anti-Christian terrorizer Saul of Tarsus.

According to the rest of Romans 8:35, tribulation or distress cannot separate you from God's love. *Distress* has to do with being in a cramped, narrow, confining, enclosed space, or to be hemmed in. This means that in those times when you feel all by yourself, when you feel life is closing in on you, as though adversaries are pressing against you and you have nowhere to turn and you feel locked in and bound up and in bondage…even that cannot separate you from God. No matter how tight it is, there's enough room in there for the presence and power of God to step in and give you enough space to feel His love.

After distress, the Bible says that persecution can't separate you from the love of God. *Persecution* means to be pursued or followed after. Those times when you feel as though you're on the run, as if the enemy is hot on your trail. Those times when it feels like you are running out of running room. There may have been many times in your life when you've felt like the devil was after you. Like things were closing in on you. You fix one problem and up pops three more. The lights go out; you fix them, and the plumbing breaks. Even in those times when it seems as though the enemy is tracking you down, those times when you're trying your best to do right, those times when you're trying to live right and follow God, yet it seems as though temptation, struggle, and sin are forever on your tail. Not even all of that can separate you from God's love, because even while you're being pursued by unrighteousness, He will never leave you nor forsake you.

CHAMPIONS DON'T RUN

Yea, though I walk through the valley of the shadow of death, I will fear no evil: for thou art with me; thy rod and thy staff they comfort me. Thou preparest a table before me in the presence of mine enemies: thou anointest my head with oil; my cup runneth over. Surely goodness and mercy shall follow me all the days of my life: and I will dwell in the house of the Lord for ever (Psalm 23:4-6).

Just try to do right and live as a champion, and a fight will find you. Once you begin to start making efforts to live a holy life, that's when temptation arrives to try to keep you from staying pure. Once you declare that you're going to get your finances straight, that's when the biggest sale of the year comes. Once you declare you're going to remain faithful to your spouse, that's when the devil brings somebody along to try to distract you. What's happening is that you are in a fight, and champions don't run from fights.

An old preacher once told me, "When you start pastoring, don't have a fighting church. But realize that sometimes if the fight comes to you, you have to fight. And if you have to fight, then fight to win." This means that you have to stop running from the enemy, and make a stand, realizing that you are endowed with the power of the living God and have already been given the victory. It is important to grasp that champions fight to celebrate the victory that *they already have in Jesus.*

Therefore, take up the full armor of God, so that you will be able to resist in the evil day, and having done everything, to stand firm. Stand firm therefore, having girded your loins with truth, and having put on the breastplate of righteousness, and having shod your feet with the preparation of the gospel of peace; in addition to all, taking up the shield of faith with which you will be able to extinguish all the flaming arrows of the evil one. And take the helmet of salvation, and the sword of the Spirit, which is the word of God (Ephesians 6:13-17 NASB).

When the battle is on, champions are equipped to take on the enemy. The visual metaphors Paul uses to describe the champion's arsenal of weapons are the belt of truth, the breastplate of righteousness, feet ready to carry the gospel of peace wherever we find ourselves, the shield of faith, the helmet of salvation, and one of the two offensive weapons available to us:

First is the sword of the Word of God. God has given us a weapon to *do damage for the Kingdom.* That offensive attack weapon is the almighty powerful *rhema* Word of the living God. And second (as noted in the verse immediately following the listing of the believer's full armor of God in Ephesians 6:13-17) is prayer:

> *...praying always with all prayer and supplication in the Spirit, being watchful to this end with all perseverance and supplication for all the saints...* (Ephesians 6:18 NKJV).

So, you've got your feet covered, you've got your heart covered, you've got your torso covered, you've got your head covered, you've got your hands covered, you've got your sword, you're ready to pray, and God says you are now ready to go into battle prepared like a champion. But wait. There's something missing from your armament. Notice that there is no protection for your back.

The book of Ephesians says to put on the *whole* armor of God, but there is no mention of protection for the back. Here's why: God doesn't need to cover up our back. There are two reasons: first, because God always has our back; and second, *He never intended for us to run from the devil!* Whenever the enemy comes at us, we are to face him head-on in the name of Jesus. Champions look the devil straight in the eye and declare, "Nothing shall separate me from the love of God!" (See Romans 8:39.)

Even way back when he was just a ruddy teenage king, before he even took the throne, David knew that the greatest weapon he had in his arsenal was God Himself. The exchange between David and Goliath tells it all:

> *The Philistine said to David, "Come to me, and I will give your flesh to the birds of the air and the beasts of the field!" Then*

David said to the Philistine, "You come to me with a sword, with a spear, and with a javelin. But I come to you in the name of the LORD of hosts, the God of the armies of Israel, whom you have defied. This day the LORD will deliver you into my hand, and I will strike you and take your head from you. And this day I will give the carcasses of the camp of the Philistines to the birds of the air and the wild beasts of the earth, that all the earth may know that there is a God in Israel" (1 Samuel 17:44-46 NKJV).

After literally prophesying Goliath's fate right to his face, David then proceeded to leave us with one of the greatest examples of how champions fearlessly rush the enemy head-on, no matter how big or bad the enemy may be:

*As the Philistine moved closer to attack him, David **ran quickly toward** the battle line to meet him. Reaching into his bag and taking out a stone, he slung it and struck the Philistine on the forehead. The stone sank into his forehead, and he fell facedown on the ground* (1 Samuel 17:48-49 NIV).

Champions don't pick fights, but they don't run from fights either!

MORE THAN CONQUERORS

David knew one key fact: champions who steadfastly follow God are more than conquerors, as apostle Paul reiterated more than a thousand years after the giant fell:

We are more than conquerors through him who loved us. For I am persuaded, that neither death nor life, nor angels nor principalities nor powers, nor things present nor things to come, nor height nor depth, nor any other created thing, shall be able to separate us from the love of God, which is in Christ Jesus our Lord (Romans 8:37-39 NKJV).

The text says that you are not merely a conqueror; you're *more than a conqueror.* This means that when you win, something else is happening behind the scenes: God has moved in your life and has taken the enemy you defeated and has caused that enemy's actions to become a *blessing* to you. This is because when God makes your enemies your footstool, after you've triumphed and won the battle, you come out stronger than you were before the trial.

Your life may have led you through many battles, but if you're reading these words right now, then you have gone through hell and won, because *you're still standing.*

How do you know you are more than a conqueror? Because God has given you complete victory. More than a conqueror is more than merely coming through; it relates to *how* you come through. You not only overcome, but you come all the way over! It means you are so destined for victory that there is no way the enemy could defeat you. It doesn't mean you won't be attacked, it means you will get victory; and when you do, the victory is amplified and intensified by the fact that you won because of your union with Christ. Every time the enemy attacks you, he gives the Lord another opportunity to defeat him through your life and your testimony. It means you not only win and come through the attack, but your victory is highlighted by another assurance that you did it by the power of the Lord working in you. You not only won, but you were *blessed by his attack*. His attack was a setup, and God gave you victory again.

Look back on the trials of your life, and I have no doubt you will see that when you came through, your head was high. When you finally won, you had your shoulders back. When you claimed victory, you were a better man, a better woman, a better employee, a better parent, a more experienced champion, with more faith and a better testimony.

My friend Dr. Marvin Sapp captures the idea of more than a conqueror in his song, "Never Could Have Made It." Marvin says, "not only did I come through, but I'm stronger. I'm wiser. I'm better; so much better." Being more than a conqueror means you not only won, but you ended up getting blessed by what you went through.

CAUSE FOR CONFIDENCE

Champions walk and talk like champions, because they know that God is always with them and He will *never* give them more than they can handle (see 1 Cor. 10:13). This promise for the champion is not cause for arrogance; it is cause for confidence. Champions have no problem telling the devil, "Come on—hit me with your best shot and see what happens to you." There is nothing that the devil will ever throw at you that you can't handle. You have already taken the devil's best punch. And if he didn't take you out last time, no matter what he throws at you next time, if you already took his worst shot, then you can take his next one. And when the smoke clears, you'll still be standing.

If you feel like God has given you an awful lot to handle in life, then be thankful that He has made you capable of handling a lot, because that is one of the great attributes of a champion.

Fret not thyself because of evildoers, neither be thou envious against the workers of iniquity. For they shall soon be cut down like the grass, and wither as the green herb. Trust in the LORD, and do good; so shalt thou dwell in the land, and verily thou shalt be fed. Delight thyself also in the LORD: and he shall give thee the desires of thine heart. Commit thy way unto the LORD; trust also in him; and he shall bring it to pass. And he shall bring forth thy righteousness as the light, and thy judgment as the noonday. Rest in the LORD, and wait patiently for him: fret not thyself because of him who prospereth in his way, because of the man who bringeth wicked devices to pass (Psalm 37:1-7).

Fret not thyself because of evil men, neither be thou envious at the wicked: for there shall be no reward to the evil man; the candle of the wicked shall be put out (Proverbs 24:19-20).

The Lord is my light and my salvation; whom shall I fear? the Lord is the strength of my life; of whom shall I be afraid? When the wicked, even mine enemies and my foes, came upon me to eat up my flesh, they stumbled and fell. Though an host should encamp against me, my heart shall not fear: though war should rise against me, in this will I be confident (Psalm 27:1-3).

God Wants to Know...

Sometimes the hardest part of my week is Sunday after church, because occasionally I find myself wondering, "Did anything happen today? Did anybody learn anything this Lord's Day? Is anybody growing? Does anybody *want* to be a better person?"

My momma used to tell me, "Son, most folk would do better if they knew better."

I don't know, Momma. Many people go to church forty or fifty times a year. They study the Word of God and hear His Word being taught and explained to them. So what? What do they *do* about the biblical facts that are taught to them? *What is their response going to be,* I often wonder, as people file out of Sunday and Wednesday services and leave the Forum and make their way home...

"We had good church today."

So, what?

"Preacher sure did preach today!"

Really? So, what did he talk about?

"I don't remember exactly what he preached on, but it sure was good!"

So, what?

"Well, I feel a little better now."

So what!

Get this: God is never as concerned about you *feeling* better than He is about you *being* better. He closely watches what you do about the revelation you receive from His Word. How you adjust, how you live, how you respond.

Ask yourself this question right now as you are reading these words on this page:

"How do I respond to the teachings I am told to observe in the Bible?"

God wants to know from each one of us the following:

- *What practical impact does My Word have on your life?*

- *What adjustments do you make in your life based on what I say?*

- *How do you change your habits and actions in accordance with what I want?*

- *What changes are you willing to make for Me?*

- *How will you reposition your life based on the revelation you receive from My Word?*

In Romans 8:28, Paul wrote that all things work together for good to them who love God. The more proper grammatical structure of that verse in today's English might state, "In all things God is at work on our behalf." God is so committed to your being a champion that everything that comes into your life God will touch with His final say. In other words, no matter what happens, it's not over until God lays His hands on it. No matter how bad it was, how hurtful it was, how painful it was, God is at work, which means that even with the worst attack that comes into your life, when God touches it, He reworks it to where it all turns out for your good. What this means for you as a champion is that your trials can lead straight to the winner's circle. No matter what trials are being hurled against you, *stand.* If a teenage sheepherder like David could defeat the entire Philistine army by taking down Goliath in the name of the Lord, then you too can be a giant slayer.

"Never tell a young person that something cannot be done."[5]

—J.A. Holmes

ENDNOTES

1. Paul's Romans 8 discourse was in response to his message of Romans 7, which pertains to our having been freed from enslavement to the law as the way to be righteous (though the law still teaches us God's moral standards).

2. The word for *predestination* is a compound word. The root word *horos* means "to mark out a boundary" or "to set limits." The prefix *pre* means "before."

3. If you have not deliberately and consciously accepted the Lord Jesus into your life, you were predestined to read this book and this very note that invites you to do so now: right where you are, simply invite the Lord Jesus into your life, ask him to fill you with His Spirit and take control of your life and make you the person He wants you to be. Your prayer may be as simple as, "Lord, save me." Or, you might say, "Jesus I believe you are the Savior and I ask you to save me now and make me your child." The specific words are not as important as the sincerity of your heart. Won't you accept Jesus now?

4. This should in no way lead you to an arrogant attitude that flaunts sin and thoughtless ungodliness. Rather, it should produce a sense of humble obedience and gratitude as you live your life for Christ. Paul was always humbled and grateful for the grace of God and the love of God that would not let him go.

5. Some sources attribute this quote to G.M. Trevelyan.

Chapter 6

The Image of a Champion

The experienced champion, once in motion, is never bewildered; once he makes his move, he is never at a loss.

—The Art of War, X.30 (paraphrased); Sun Tzu

A T the age of seven, Glenn Cunningham had the responsibility of going to the little country schoolhouse and firing up the potbellied stove to warm the room before class began. One morning his teacher and classmates arrived to discover the entire school engulfed in flames. Glenn was pulled from the burning building unconscious and near death, with severe third-degree burns over the lower half of his body. He survived, but the fire claimed his brother's life.

The doctor's prognosis was bleak. He told Glenn's mother that the boy would surely die. Glenn defied the odds and began a slow recovery. Yet, he overheard the doctor tell his mother that although Glenn didn't die, he would be a cripple for the rest of his life. Nearly a year after the blazing schoolhouse fire that killed his brother and almost claimed his own life and made him a cripple, Glenn Cunningham learned to walk again.

"By the grace of God," Cunningham said, "I learned to run again."

Cunningham refused to believe a doctor's negative assessment. Although he had no feeling in his legs, it wasn't long before he began to walk again, and eventually to run. And finally, one day, he became a world-class athlete.

The image of a champion is varied. Like Glenn Cunningham, champions are overcomers, conquerors, achievers. They also are both followers *and* leaders. Champions are warriors *and* ambassadors. True champions are true servants. This is because champions are conformed to the image of God's Son (see Romans 8:29), the Champion of all champions.

Some of the greatest athletes had to overcome obstacles on their way to being conformed to the image of a champion. Michael Jordan was cut from his junior high school basketball squad and still went on to become perhaps the greatest player ever to take the court. Jim Abbott lost an arm as a child and still became an outstanding major league baseball pitcher. Jackie Robinson overcame severe racial prejudice and still not only played in baseball's major leagues, but was also named Rookie of the Year. Lance Armstrong had testicular cancer that spread to his brain and he beat the cancer *and* won an unprecedented seven Tour de France bicycling titles.

There is a dangerous theology out there today that teaches that if you're really right with God, then you won't be struggling—that you'll get every prayer answered, that you'll see miracles from sunup to sundown, drive the best car, wear the best clothes, name it and claim it and frame it and blab it and grab it; but that if you're struggling, weak, or unaccomplished, then you must be somehow living outside of the will of God. That distorted image of biblical truth implies that every "true" Christian should be living a life of comfort and ease. Obviously, that's untrue. Otherwise Jesus Himself would not have said in John 16:33, "In the world ye shall have tribulation: but be of good cheer; I have overcome the world" (John 16:33). Nor would apostle Paul have given his Romans 5:3-4 encouragement for us to "rejoice in our sufferings, because we know that suffering produces perseverance; perseverance, character; and character, hope" (Rom. 5:3-4 NIV).

The simple fact is, *champions overcome.* But they overcome *something.* They have victory over *something.* They are conquerors over *something.* I think the reality of the champion spirit is seen in Second Chronicles 20 where Jehoshaphat is facing the enemy. I love what the Lord says to him. In verse 15 the prophet tells him that "the battle is not yours, but God's" (2 Chron. 20:15). And then in the very next verse he says, "tomorrow you are to go down against them" (see 2 Chron. 20:16). Whoa! If the battle is the Lord's, then it seems like we ought to be able to sit back and watch the Lord win "His" battle. But not so. God says, "The battle is Mine, and I will give you victory, but you must take the battlefield."

The truth is that God gives us victory, but that victory comes when we stand against the enemy, when we engage the enemy. God then gives us the victory that has already been won. However, we win when we stand *against* something. The promise of God is not that there will be no battle, but that we will gain victory in the battle.

THE REAL DEAL ABOUT REAL CHAMPIONS

A man once sent me a bookmark on which was printed, *I will face nothing today that God and I cannot handle*. But satan has sold us a bill of goods, which is that we're in trouble because we're not smart enough; we grew up on the wrong side of the tracks; we will never amount to anything. Just as God is recruiting us for His dream team, satan is trying to sideline us. That is why we must adjust our thinking. Champions recognize that life moves from one challenge to the next. They believe they will face hurdles, but never one they cannot clear. They know they will face mountains, but never one they cannot climb. They will encounter valleys, but never one they cannot go through; nor a Red Sea they cannot cross. Champions never assume lack of opposition; they simply assume victory over every opposition.

It has been said that success is 80 percent attitude and 20 percent aptitude, because the greatest opposition you will ever face to fulfilling your personal dream begins in your own mind. Champions develop the mind of Christ, which says, "I can do all things through Christ who strengthens me" (Phil. 4:13 NKJV). The devil will attack you at every opportunity, because as the Bible says, "The thief does not come except to steal, and to kill, and to destroy" (John 10:10 NKJV). But you have authority over satan because of who you are in Christ.

I am on the battlefield for my Lord. I'm on the battlefield for my Lord, and I promised Him that I would serve Him 'til I die; I'm on the battlefield for my Lord.

—*On the Battlefield*, Sylvana Bell and E.V. Banks

When you're on the battlefield for God, you're not wearing the uniform of a soldier just for the looks. It amazes me how many Christians are surprised and get offended when they are attacked. Yesterday they were soldiers in the army of the Lord, dancing all day long, praising the Lord with shouts of glee; but today a little bitty wave comes along in their lives, and they flip out, moaning and crying and wailing.

Far too many believers are one tragedy away from giving up on God. A distorted theology paints a false image that causes people to be poorly equipped to handle the realities of life. They're in as long as the sun is shining, the music is playing, and they're shouting, "Hallelujah!" But hit hard times—when jobs are going overseas, the rich seem to be getting richer, the middle class struggling not to slide lower, cities being ravaged by economic downslide, health insurance not covering what you were told it would cover, foreclosures and credit debt skyrocketing—and they're out, huddling shell-shocked in a corner as if things like that just don't happen to Christians.

I know people who have turned from God because they lost their job. I know some who have left the Lord because of bad marriages. I know others who have turned their backs on Him because they couldn't find a husband. I know a lady who turned from the Lord because she found out her husband was gay. I know another who deserted God because she couldn't find a man at all. Many believers live a life of divine delusions. Their concept of God is shaped more by their carnal expectations as put forth by a secular culture than by a biblical portrait of the Lord as revealed in His word.

Champions always assume they will be attacked—they know earth is a battlefield. We're in a fight, and the enemy prowls around looking for every opportunity to knock God's people off. Soldiers don't freak out when they get shot at—it's the enemy's job description to shoot at the followers of God. Just go to the examples of heroes like Job, the Reverend Martin Luther King Jr., the apostle Paul, Anne Frank, the prophet Elijah, John the Baptist, and on and on throughout history.

CHAMPIONS SOMETIMES DEFEAT THEMSELVES

One of my biggest heroes is the great King David. One of the ways champions become champions is by defeating a champion, and David defeated a Philistine champion named Goliath. David was still a teenage sheepherder when he slew Goliath, a trained warrior who stood more than nine feet tall.

David became a giant killer before he even took the kingship of Israel. Yet, read the lament of this great giant-slaying champion many years later, after the prophet Nathan brought David's shameful iniquity with Bathsheba to light:

O Lord, do not rebuke me in Your wrath, nor chasten me in Your hot displeasure! For Your arrows pierce me deeply, and Your hand presses me down. There is no soundness in my flesh because of Your anger, nor any health in my bones because of my sin. For my iniquities have gone over my head; like a heavy burden they are too heavy for me (Psalm 38:1-4 NKJV).

David told the Lord he was struggling with His displeasure of him, that he was living under the load of God's anger against him because of what he had done. David was a champion, yet he said, "My guilt has overwhelmed me like a burden too heavy to bear" (Psalm 38:4 NIV). David was a champion who was struggling with the weight of guilt due to deliberate and outrageous sin; a guilt that kindled the anger of God against him.

You may have experienced times when you felt like God was mad at you. Times when you looked back at your life, examined your choices, reviewed your mistakes, traced your tracks, and were reminded of how you had messed up. And in the wake of having sinned against God, you realized that you needed to go to Him. David was saying to God that when he sensed his need to go to Him, the problem was that he knew what he had done and he was carrying a load of guilt over it. And he knew that although he had to go to God, he also knew that God was mad at him—and that both scared him and crushed him. *I've let you down, Lord.*

There are times when even champions feel defeated and want to give up. In this setting, David appeared to be drowning in a cesspool of his own guilt and iniquity. He felt like he couldn't handle the torment of his transgressions. He felt a separation from God his Rock. He struggled with the fact that what he did had caused God to get mad at him. It was a heavy load that seemed too much to bear.

In Psalm 38:5 David said, "My wounds stink and are corrupt because of my foolishness." Perhaps you have had someone important to you who looked at something you'd done, and you wondered what kind of blame fool you must have been to have gone and done that kind of a thing. You know you did it, and you're wondering what in the world you must have been on to make you make such a fool decision as that. Sometimes you don't have to wait for somebody to call you a fool. Just look at your crazy self in the mirror; you know what you did.

David is saying, essentially, "I'm freaking out because of my own foolishness!" In the secret places of our own spirit, there are times when we are just like David, wallowing in a sea of guilt. And because of our guilt, we sense God's "hot displeasure." In those times, it's easy to become paranoid, because whenever things start to seem a little off, you begin to wonder if it is payback time. That was the battle being waged in David's mind—this champion who had defeated the fearsome Goliath of Gath.

I cannot tell you how many times I have wallowed in a sea of my own guilt. I can't even count how many times I have walked in paranoia that the retribution of what I did would come upon my children or on theirs. I'm talking about generational effects, about a fear that if retribution doesn't come in your time, it might come upon your children or grandchildren, and it's all your fault. You live your life under the weight of that guilt.

David said, "My sin is ever before me" (Psalm 51:3). Every time he tried to get away from it, something jumped up and reminded him. I can't imagine how apostle Paul lived with the burden of the memory of having delivered Christians up for death and imprisonment, and of even serving as an accomplice in the stoning death of Stephen when he was Saul of Tarsus.

My wife and I have been married for more than thirty years. When we had been married for around ten years, at the start of my second year of teaching at a Christian college, I was notified that my contract was not going to be renewed, because I had once been divorced many years earlier. The matter was ancient history, repented of before God, forgiven, buried, and covered under the blood of Jesus, but was now being resurrected and used against me in my current position at the university. After I was fired, I thought I was finished. My heart was broken because my life had truly turned around. I was living for God and trying to do better. Things were going pretty well. I had assumed that my old life was history—until the moment I was told that my services were no longer needed, due to a long-forgiven sin.

I was stunned when that man said, "We will not be renewing your contract."

"But sir," I responded, "that was twelve or fifteen years ago. It's long over."

"I'm sorry, Doctor," he said, "but the word from the main office was that we cannot renew your contract." And they fired me.

That's exactly what satan does. He digs up our past and our old sins and blatantly parades them before everyone. That's the reality of the life of a champion. My old college would never have allowed Saul to become the apostle Paul and would have dethroned David the moment they heard about Bathsheba—abruptly ending God's plan for the Messiah to come through King David's lineage.

You may have experienced the pain of divorce. You might have even spent time behind bars. You may have stayed in a halfway house because of a drug or alcohol addiction. You may have gotten fired for some indiscretion. You might have become pregnant when you weren't married. But now you're trying to turn your life around. You've made a new start. And then someone pulls your file and uncovers your "history." It's as though you can't progress beyond your past and the guilt of what you did, because who you used to be has come back to haunt you. In times like those, throwing in the towel seems like the only option. For the champion, there will always be opportunities to quit. That's just reality. You will face struggles.

CHAMPIONS FEEL

Awake! Why do You sleep, O Lord? Arise! Do not cast us off for-ever. Why do You hide Your face, and forget our affliction and our oppression? For our soul is bowed down to the dust; our body clings to the ground. Arise for our help, and redeem us for Your mercies' sake (Psalm 44:23-26 NKJV).

Have you ever felt like God couldn't hear you? Like He is too busy for you? My problem is that my theology sometimes messes with me because I've studied and trained to be a scholar. As a scholar, I know that God is omnipotent and omnipresent; He sees all and knows all. But when you're in the middle of a mess and your prayers don't seem to rise any higher than the ceiling, and the heavens seem to have turned into brass and nothing is being resolved, theology doesn't count for a heck of a lot. When life is in your face and you're going through the wringer, all those Scriptures don't meet your needs. When you feel like your needs aren't being met, for someone to come along and beat you down with Bible verses is certainly not productive.

Too often, some Christians play holy games and act all spiritually deep and come across as if they're getting all of their own prayers answered, but their problem is that they're so deep in it, they're stuck in it. I know of people who have been hanging in there, praying for a long time for something, and haven't received an answer yet, but they still love and trust Jesus, because they are champions.

Although David knew that God hears all and sees all, he felt as though God was asleep and couldn't hear him. He said, essentially, "Lord, why are You asleep?" It's during those trying times that you feel God cannot hear you. Your spiritual intellect tells you that He hears all and sees all; He sits high and looks low. But your emotions tell you He has abandoned you.

I love how Gideon expressed it:

"But sir," Gideon replied, "if the Lord is with us, why has all this happened to us? Where are all his wonders that our fathers told us about when they said, 'Did not the Lord bring us up out of Egypt?' But now the Lord has abandoned us and put us into the hand of Midian" (Judges 6:13 NIV).

Sometimes it seems like God is blessing everyone but you. Don't be ashamed; don't be afraid. Even Gideon, whom the angel of the Lord called a "mighty man of valour" (Judges 6:12), wondered where God was. If God is for us, then where are all the miracles? It's like the Lord is asleep and isn't answering prayers. He can't hear anything from you, and you can't hear anything from Him.

Look at this beautiful response in the Psalm:

He will not suffer thy foot to be moved: he that keepeth thee will not slumber. Behold, he that keepeth Israel shall neither slumber nor sleep. The Lord is thy keeper: the Lord is thy shade upon thy right hand (Psalm 121:3-5).

The revelation of the Psalm 44 text is this: David felt like God was asleep. His personal reality was his personal reality—it was *not* divine truth, but that's the way he felt. That's how champions feel sometimes too. In spite of a distorted picture that the world and the Church give us about what a champion should look like—good cheer and red roses all the time—here is the real deal about real champions: just because you're going through a trial doesn't mean you're less than a champion. There isn't necessarily something wrong with you because you had a rough day. It doesn't mean you've drifted away from God, or Him away from you.

Job is another champion who faced unimaginable physical and mental torment and grief over losing his livelihood, his health, his wealth, and his entire family in an extremely short period of time for no obvious reason:

Oh that I knew where I might find Him! that I might come even to His seat! I would order my cause before Him, and fill my mouth with arguments. I would know the words which He would answer me, and understand what He would say unto me. Will He plead against me with His great power? No; but He would put strength in me. There the righteous might dispute with Him; so should I be delivered for ever from my judge. Behold, I go forward, but He is not there; and backward, but I cannot perceive Him (Job 23:3-8).

Notice how Job sounds like a psalmist? My translation for Job 23:3 would be, "I wish I knew where to find God! If somebody could just tell me where to find Him. If only I knew where He went."

Look at Job 23:8: "I go forward, but he is not there; and backward, but I cannot perceive him." There have been times when I've felt exactly like that. Not just on a Thursday or Friday night, but some Sunday mornings right in the pulpit, in the presence of the saints. I'm a champion, but a human champion struggling with my flesh. I have experienced times when the choir is singing, and the band is jamming, and it seems like everybody can see and touch and feel the Lord but me. But I soldier on. That's what champions do.

Job is saying that there are times when even a real champion feels as though he or she can't find God. There are times in the life of a champion when you feel distant from God, when you look for Him and can't find Him. If you have ever felt like the anointing of the Holy Ghost was falling on everybody but you, then welcome to the club—you're human like the rest of us. We've all felt that.

Here's the interesting thing: Job had not sinned. David knew he had messed up. But if you go all the way back to chapter 1 of Job, you'll discover that Job didn't do anything wrong. I'm not saying he was perfect, but he lived his life in accordance with God's instructions. He made consistent effort to walk upright in the ways of Jehovah. He prayed. He helped other people. In fact, it appeared as though he had done everything right. He even made sacrifices to God *just in case* his kids had sinned and he wasn't aware of it. Yet, satan got permission from God to test Job, and he set out to rock Job's entire world. And suddenly, from right out of left field,

Job was blindsided by disaster and destruction, and he wondered, *Where in the world did all this come from?*

Job was a real champion and had probably lived a cleaner life than King David did, but these two champions had one thing in common: "Where are you, God? I can't find You." Yet, when it seemed Job was about to throw in the towel on his search for God, he made this statement:

> *But He knows the way that I take; when He has tested me, I shall come forth as gold* (Job 23:10 NKJV).

Thank God for the theology of "but." I know I've been here for a long time, *but I shall.* I had to cry sometimes, *but I shall overcome.* I had to stand all by myself, *but I shall come forth.* Weeping may endure for a night *but* joy comes in the morning (see Ps. 30:5). "Even the youths shall faint and be weary, and the young men shall utterly fall, *but* they that wait upon the Lord shall renew their strength" (Isa. 40:30-31). "*But* my God shall supply all your need according to his riches in glory by Christ Jesus" (Phil. 4:19). Thank God for the "but."

You may not know when or how long it will take to come out victorious, but like Job, there is something better on the other side of your ordeal. When you can't see or hear God, your faith tells you that He knows what you're going through and how you're feeling. He knows the lies and innuendos being spread about you, and He gives you this promise:

> *For we do not have a high priest who cannot sympathize with our weaknesses, but One who has been tempted in all things as*

we are, yet without sin. Therefore, let us draw near with confidence to the throne of grace, so that we may receive mercy and find grace to help in time of need (Hebrews 4:15-16 NASB).

Job held on because something inside him assured him that on the other side of his crushing trial awaited a power-packed testimony.

I have lost track of how many times the devil has come against me. But there's a champion in me that knows that every obstacle is just another opportunity for me to clear the hurdle. Every Red Sea is an opportunity for God to open the waves and let me walk through on dry land. Every Philippian jail is an opportunity for me to praise Him and thank Him and watch the shackles fall off in the name of Jesus.

Sometimes you have to look yourself in the mirror and firmly say to yourself, "Self, you are a champion! And you are going to come out of this on top and emerge in the winner's circle, in Jesus' name!" If nobody claps for you, if nobody gives you a standing ovation, clap for yourself and plow forward. Tell yourself, "You *go!*" Because God is with you.

IT'S TIME TO RUN AGAIN!

I'm personally acquainted with many champions at Faithful Bible Central Church. Donald is one such champion. Donald was shot in the neck and wasn't supposed to live, let alone be able to talk. Now, every once in awhile when I look out in the pews and see Donald ministering, I notice that some people are cringing at the hoarseness of his voice. But every time Donald opens his mouth, it's a testimony of glory to Jesus.

Another champion is Frankie, a cancer survivor who passed away after bouncing back from cancer for years. Sometimes people raised their eyebrows when he began to run around the floor of the Forum. In those times, he was celebrating because he was an over-comer—you couldn't keep Frankie down.

I once stood at the bedside of a champion named Pam just before she had surgery to have a brain tumor removed. The doctors told her she might not make it, and that even if she did, the outlook was grim. But Pam is still standing and still fighting, because she stood strong in her faith in the Word of God.

After suffering unimaginable burns and prognoses of death from his doctors, professional runner Glenn Cunningham went on to become one of the greatest athletes in history, setting the world record in the one-mile run in 1934. He was a champion whose destiny at one time seemed to be confining him to a wheelchair. Yet, the heart of a champion beat within Glenn Cunningham, driving him to choose a different course—one that astonished his doctors, his family and his friends, and now serves as a powerful example to us all.

The image of real champions is one of people who *do not quit.* Their faith will not allow it.

But without faith it is impossible to please Him: for he that cometh to God must believe that He is, and that He is a rewarder of them that diligently seek Him (Hebrews 11:6).

You may have been hurt by someone in church. You may have been passed by for a promotion. You may still bear the emotional and physical scars of past abuse. You might have suffered loneliness and rejection from family or friends. You may feel like God's presence has escaped you. But like Job, maintain your faith. God still sees you. Persevere a little longer and seek Him a little closer, and He will reveal Himself to you—and powerfully so, for He does not desert His champions…

*I am with you **always**, even unto the end of the world* (Matthew 28:20).

Chapter 7

No Lone Rangers

THE original Dream Team, the U.S. basketball squad that won the gold medal at the 1992 Olympics in Barcelona, was arguably the greatest team ever assembled in sports. Team USA cruised past the competition, dominated the court, and beat its opponents like a drum in eight consecutive games—by an average of *44 points* per game. It was a classic blowout. The effect of this historical moment was a dramatic increase in the popularity of basketball around the world.

But the team's greatest feat was that, for the first time, a group of players was assembled that included professional NBA all-stars, combining the talents of athletic champions such as Michael Jordan, Larry Bird, Charles Barkley, Patrick Ewing, and Magic Johnson, just to name a few.

> "It was like Elvis and the Beatles put together. Traveling with the Dream Team was like traveling with twelve rock stars. That's all I can compare it to."
>
> —Coach Chuck Daly

Part of my call as a pastor is to be a coach of champions, and it is my desire to exemplify the traits of the greatest Coach of all time, Jesus Christ. You may be ever so gifted and anointed, but there are no lone rangers in the Body of Christ, because God will never call you to do or to be what you could do all on your own. Whatever He calls you to do will require that you be a part of some form of team effort. For example, one player doesn't make an entire football team. A company is built with more than one employee. A family is not just one person. Even a motion picture may have had just one writer, but it took a huge production team to bring the words on the pages to life on the big screen. Even a church is a body (see Eph. 4:16), made up of many members. You can't build a ministry by yourself. You can't work for the Kingdom all by yourself. And you cannot be victorious all on your own. All that God will ever call you to do will require that you be a part of a *team*.

Over the past few decades a narcissistic, self-centeredness has crept into the Body of Christ. There has been a disturbing theological shift emphasizing the individual. And yet, the revelation of Scripture is very clear that we are a part of, and related to, all other believers. There are no lone rangers in the Kingdom of heaven, as apostle Paul alluded to in his letter to the Corinthians:

*Apollos and I are working as a **team**, with the same aim, though each of us will be rewarded for his own hard work* (1 Corinthians 3:8 TLB).

RECRUITING CHAMPIONS

He went up on the mountain and called to Him those He Himself wanted. And they came to Him. Then He appointed twelve, that they might be with Him and that He might send them out to preach (Mark 3:13-14 NKJV).

Jesus was the all-time expert at enlisting individual members who possessed the right stuff to help advance His Father's cause. He was out to create a championship team out of regular guys. One of the primary responsibilities of a coach is to recruit members onto the team. Let's take a look at how Coach Jesus began the recruitment of His team, the model He left for us to follow, and the mandate He gives us as champions...

First, Jesus called to Himself those He wanted, and they came to Him. The Mark 3 text says that He called a group to Him (see Mark 3:13). In Matthew 22:14, Jesus said, "Many are called, but few are chosen." The idea is that the opportunity is available to everyone, but few will rise to the challenge of the call, and not all of the candidates called will want to be on the team. And, the coach might discover, some of those called will turn out not to be right for the team.

Next, out of the group Jesus called, He chose twelve. One version says He "appointed" twelve (see Mark 3:14 NKJV). Thus, Jesus called and appointed (or "ordained") twelve. In Matthew 4:19, Jesus said, "Follow me, and I will make you fishers of men" (Matt. 4:19; see also Mark 1:17). The phrase *I will make*[1] means the same thing as the words *ordain* and *appoint*. What Jesus did was take twelve individuals and make them into a unit of one. *"The* twelve," in fact, is stated nearly three dozen times in the New Testament—one unit of twelve men brought together from all walks of life as a team that was about to change the world profoundly and permanently.

On February 22, 1980, during the 1980 Winter Olympics, the U.S. men's hockey team became known as the Miracle on Ice for making a gold medal run at Team CCCP (the former Soviet Union). When team coach Herb Brooks was questioned about his selection of the players for the American squad, he said, "I'm not looking for the best players. I'm looking for the right ones."

Brooks chose his team in a similar way to Jesus. The team of scrappy college kids didn't even consist of the best hockey players America had to offer. As individuals, they were solid players, but the team wasn't even supposed to finish in the medals. Yet, it was as a *team* that, in the final game, the seventh-seed brash, young Americans defeated the mighty Soviets and took the gold.

"A good coach will make his players see what they can be, rather than what they are."

—Ara Parseghian, Notre Dame football coach

THE RECRUITMENT STRATEGY OF JESUS

Jesus had an odd way of recruiting that is antithetical to the way recruitment is approached in professional sports today. Let's look at the recruitment pattern of the Lord:

*Brothers, think of what you were when you were called. Not many of you were **wise by human standards**; not many* *were **influential**; not many were of **noble birth**. But God chose **the foolish things of the world to shame the wise**; God chose **the weak things of the world to shame the strong**. He chose **the lowly things of this world and the despised things**—and **the things that are not**—to **nullify the things that are*** (1 Corinthians 1:26-28 NIV).

The strange thing about the recruitment strategy of Jesus was that He chose the most unlikely. The Scripture above indicates that some who were wise were called, some who were strong, some who were influential, some who were noble. Some of those who Jesus handpicked were successful businessmen. But when He called those who were, in the eyes of their contemporaries, wise, those who were mighty, who were connected, who were powerful, they soon began to learn that they weren't as wise as they *could* be. Not as strong as they *could* be. Had not yet accomplished all they *could* do. He said, basically, to these men, "You haven't gone as far as you can go. You haven't become all you can be. There is yet something greater still to pull out of you." The lesson is that Jesus can take *any* willing recruits from *any* strata of society—high, medium, or low— and make them champions.

Tom Mullins, pastor of Christ Fellowship Church in Palm Beach Gardens, Florida, used to coach football at Georgetown College in Kentucky. One time he was considering recruiting a young man from Mississippi for the team. After reading the kid's profile, Mullins decided that he probably wasn't going to select the young man, who stood only six feet one inch tall and weighed around 220. He wasn't quite big enough for Georgetown. But even though Coach Mullins had pretty much written the kid off as too small and unqualified, he still went to visit the boy and pay him a courtesy call.

The first thing Coach Mullins noticed when he walked into the young man's house was that his father was six feet seven inches tall, weighed 255 pounds, and had huge feet. A few minutes later, the mother treaded into the room. She stood at least six feet two inches tall and weighed probably 200 or so, and her feet were about as big as her husband's. The coach looked at the teenage boy and realized that with parents like these, the kid had potential. Mullins thought, *If his momma is this big and his daddy is this big, this young man isn't finished growing yet.* So he changed his mind and recruited the boy, who, in just two more years, grew to six feet seven inches tall and weighed in at 260 pounds.

Coach Mullins didn't recruit that boy for who he was. He recruited him for who he would become.

Not everybody who comes to Jesus has been down and out. There are a few people who know nothing about being down. He sends the call even to those who seem to have it all and have it all together—because *everyone* has more room to grow.

Most of us, however, fall under First Corinthians 1:27, where it says, essentially, "He chooses the weak" (see 1 Cor. 1:27). He does that for a very specific purpose. When the draft comes around in professional sports each season, the best players are chosen in the first-round draft pick, then the best remaining for the second-round, and so on, choosing from the cream of the crop for the upcoming season. Those top-pick athletes generally go to the weakest teams. It is then expected that those teams will improve and become stronger, because they now have the best athletes.

When the team's record is improved, everybody knows that the reason is because they got the best of the crop.

But Jesus didn't do it that way, because He doesn't play by our rules. In fact, He did just the opposite, because His thoughts are not our thoughts, nor are His ways our ways. In the same way that the heavens are higher than the earth, so are God's ways higher than our ways, and His thoughts than our thoughts (see Isa. 55:8-9). To create His winning team, Jesus recruited the weakest, least experienced players—those whom you'd never picture as rising up to the challenge and then going on to create a dynasty that in two millennia would grow to a couple of billion followers throughout the world.

Jesus chooses the least likely folks—those whom no one else would choose; the ones who have flaws, weaknesses, and struggles, those who haven't yet arrived—in order to confound and put to shame the mighty so that *no* flesh can glory in His sight (see 1 Cor. 1:29). He chooses people who messed up in the past, made some bad choices, went down some rough roads, picked some wrong partners. He chooses those who weren't supposed to win. Folks who didn't get picked in the draft. Those who got injured in the game. Jesus chooses these people and then turns around and puts them on the team. Jesus does this in such a way that when He gets through, nobody can always pat the same player on the back. One player doesn't make the team the winner; the *team* makes each player a winner.

When Jesus enlisted the twelve disciples, they were a rough bunch. None of them were rabbis, nor had any of them sat under rabbinical training. They weren't temple leaders. They had never run a ministry. None ever went on a mission trip. But after three and a half years of personal coaching under the Master, they were just about ready to take the world by storm. The final touch was when the Holy Spirit came upon them; then they took the field and entered the battle. And the world has never been the same since.

There is another reason in professional sports that the team which ends the season with the worst record is given the opportunity to choose first among the best players available for the next season. It is not only so the team can be more competitive the following year, but also so the fans won't get frustrated and bored with perpetual, lopsided blowouts during the playing season. This points out another difference in thinking between Jesus and the norm: Jesus doesn't want an even playing field against the enemy. He doesn't want us to win a few and lose a few against the devil and his team of fallen angels. Jesus wants us to be the champions in fight after fight. He wants a blowout every single match. He wants victory in every battle.

Normally you would think that His desire to win every contest against the enemy would be a reason Jesus should recruit only the best for the team. *Wrong.* He wants every one of us to get in the game—not just the best, the brightest, the most capable, but *everyone.*

Life on earth is a full-contact battle, where the devil seeks whom he may devour (see 1 Pet. 5:8) and where he wants only to kill, steal, and destroy (see John 10:10). The battle is 24/7 here on planet Earth, and God doesn't want *anyone* sitting out the game. That's why His game plan allows Him to take even the worst recruits and turn them into champions who go out *as one* and pound the enemy to dust beneath their feet.

Champions only enter into alliances when they have the same mindset as their teammates.

—*The Art of War*, VII.12 (paraphrased); Sun Tzu

CHAMPIONS HANG OUT WITH CHAMPIONS

An interesting thing about champions is that they tend to hang out with other champions. I didn't say they hang out with perfect people. I said they hang out with champions. For example, unless he's playing with kids at a charity event, basketball great Kobe Bryant no longer plays parking lot basketball down the road. Now he only plays on a certain level, with his fellow pros. Because champions hang with champions.

If you run with those who've already achieved something, they'll draw out the champion in you that is waiting to bust out. When you gather with godly champions, the atmosphere becomes charged with the presence of the Lord and ignited by the power of His Word to the point where God expands your capacity to be a champion. You breathe the air of victory. You inhale in the atmosphere of winners.

It's like the story (told with many variations) of a man who owned a mule and lived near the Kentucky Derby. Each year during the Derby he would take his mule to the practice sessions and watch the thoroughbreds be put through their paces. This man and his mule became a fixture around Churchill Downs.

One day one of the trainers asked him, "Why do you keep on bringing that mule to the Kentucky Derby? Don't you know mules can't run in the Derby? Matter'a fact, mules can't even try out to enter the Kentucky Derby."

"Yeah," the man answered, "I know that."

The trainer responded, "Well, if you know your mule will never run in the Derby, then why do you continue to bring it here in the presence of all of these finely bred thoroughbreds and champions?"

The man answered, "I know this here mule may never run in the Kentucky Derby. But I bring him here every year so he can hang out with the thoroughbreds, because I figure even if he doesn't run, the exposure will do him good."

You may never run your Kentucky Derby or become an Olympic athlete, but just the exposure of being around people who know what it's like to be down and get back up and win will do you good. Just to be able to hang out with someone who has been financially bankrupt or unemployed and is now debt free and owns a new house will revive the spirit of the champion within you. The exposure of being around somebody who has been through danger, toil, and snares and triumphed over them all, will do you well.

THE CHAMPION IN YOU WAS MADE TO WIN

There's nothing more frustrating than to see a professional athlete sidelined because of an injury. Every now and then during a televised game, the camera will zoom in on an athlete sitting on the sidelines and you can see the anxiety on the player's face, brought on by the frustration of sitting on the bench unable to do anything for the team. Champions want nothing more than to get back in the game and experience the thrill of victory. But when champions are sidelined, there's a kind of desperation that overcomes them, because *champions were made to win*. And you can't win unless you get back in the game.

If you've been off the field and away from the game, it's time to put yourself back in. I don't care how many games you may have lost, it's time to get back out there. I don't care how many struggles you may have gone through, it's time to get back on the field.

Isn't it interesting that no matter what the score was last week, when a team comes out of the locker room for the next game, it always comes out with a new excitement and enthusiasm and an anticipation that this is the game where it's all going to get better than ever before? This is the game they're going to win by a land-slide. This is the game that's going to start the victory march to the championship—and start a dynasty.

I believe one of the reasons Jesus chose so many flawed men to be on His team is because it says to others, "Man, if God can use *him*, He can sure use me!" Our praise team often sings a song that is a prayer that says, "If you can use anything, Lord, you can use me."

BUILD AND DEPLOY

Mark 3:14 says that Jesus called the disciples that they might be with Him and that He might send them out (see Mark 3:14). He called them to Him in order to build them and deploy them.

My job as a pastor and a teacher, according to Ephesians 4:12, is to equip you and to build you up so that you will know there is a champion in you and so you will be prepared to go out. Not just to go out to church. As dramatic and exciting as church can be, church is not the playing field; it's just the practice field. The real court, the real field, is outside the church walls, out in the streets, in the cities, among the people. The real game is not what you do behind closed doors. The real game is what you do after and before church. It's not what you do after the praise and worship; it's what you do after the benediction. It's not how holy and righteous you are when the saints are gathered and the choir is singing; it's how holy and righteous you are after the service is over, after the lights are turned off, after you leave the building.

Champions are as righteous on Sunday morning as they are on Friday night. Anybody can be holy on Sunday morning. But the real game is *out there*, in the world. Church is simply a station of release, a deployment area. It's where you go to learn the game plan. It's where you go to study the playbook. It's where you go to look at those who have gone on before, who have overcome every obstacle they faced. God calls you to the gathering place of your church only to release you from that place out into the world, where the rubber hits the road, where the devil prowls about seeking to knock off God's children. God calls you out there to use you as a champion, because it's only *out there* that you truly become a champion.

Looking at those whom God chose for His team helps you to see that there's a place for you as a champion on God's team. Noah was a champion, but he used to be a drunk. Abraham was a champion, yet he used to be a liar. David was a champion, and he was once an adulterer. Jesus doesn't choose those with perfect, winning seasons. If He only chose those who had perfect records, we could dismiss the entire New Testament, because then those "perfect" people could take all the credit. Everyone has sinned. Everyone has fallen short of the glory of God. Every single person will miss the mark sooner or later. But the amazing power of God is that He can still use you on His team. In fact, He *wants* you on the team.

God is recruiting you today. He wants to make you into a champion. He wants to take you beyond your past and into the potential of your future. There may be things in your life that would seem to disqualify you from the team. But it doesn't matter what your life has been. It doesn't matter how many games you may have lost in the past. It doesn't even matter how many games you may have won in the past. God never looks at you for who you are, or even for what you used to be. He looks at you for what you *can be* when He gets through laying His hands on your life. He calls you for the potential and giftings within you that haven't even risen to the surface yet. He looks at you right now and says, "I can use you," because He calls you *for who you are becoming*. And here is a glimpse of what you will be like:

> *Beloved, now we are children of God; and it has not yet been revealed what we shall be, but we know that when He is revealed, **we shall be like Him** (1 John 3:2 NKJV).*

ENDNOTE

1. Not to be confused with poieo (to make as in create). "I will make you" means to make something out of something that already exists; whereas, "In the beginning God created" means to make something out of nothing (creatio ex nihilo, or "creation out of nothing").

Chapter 8

Champions Understand Success

G OD'S will is that you are successful. But success doesn't just happen. Ask any champion. It requires preparation and perseverance to accomplish your goals and dreams. Yet, in the King James Version of the Bible, there is only *one* place where the word *success* appears:

> *This book of the law shall not depart out of thy mouth; but thou shalt meditate therein day and night, that thou mayest observe to do according to all that is written therein: for then thou shalt make thy way prosperous, and **then thou shalt have good success*** (Joshua 1:8).

The context of the passage above is the preparation of Israel to move into the Promised Land. God speaks to the nation and says, basically, "Do these things, and you will be successful."

God did not make you and save you just for you to be a failure in the world. It is important that you understand that it is God's will that you succeed. That is a truth that champions not only believe, but that they also pass on to their children. It does not matter where we come from. Our economic, racial, or social status does not matter. God does not make junk. He did not make you to fail.

Back when I began in ministry, several pastors said to me, "Son, God did not call you to be a success. He only called you to be faithful."

I thought that was pretty deep and spiritual, and I knew they were right about faith. But what grabbed my attention was that they said it's not important to succeed. So I asked one of them, "Well, sir, does that mean we're supposed to fail?"

"Of course not," he answered.

"Then what does the Bible say about us succeeding?" I wanted to know.

"Well," he responded, "God doesn't really say much about that."

So, for years I labored under the misconception that succeeding was not important to God. And then one day I messed up and actually *studied* the Bible. And I discovered that success *is* clearly, specifically, and often included in the economy of God's Kingdom. God called us to be faithful, yes, but we are successful *to the degree that we are faithful*. In fact, faith helps to form the definition of success, because without faith, you might never even attempt to achieve what God tells you to do.

WHAT IS SUCCESS?

Webster's New Collegiate Dictionary defines *success* as "favorable termination of a venture; a desired outcome of something attempted; a prosperous or advantageous issue."[1]

If God did not want us to be successful in our ventures, He would not have given us such plain instructions about how to be successful. In the Joshua text, God tells us that if we do certain things in specific ways, then we will have good success. There are revelations and instructions in Scripture as to how we can become successful, because success is an important part of God's will. You don't build a kingdom on lack of success.

Let's look at a working, biblical definition from various Scripture verses relevant to the topic of success. First, this passage from Ecclesiastes:

> *Whatever your hand finds to do, do it with your might; for there is no work or device or knowledge or wisdom in the grave where you are going* (Ecclesiastes 9:10 NKJV).

In our vernacular, the Scripture above would say *work while you can*. Whatever your hand finds to do, do it with all your might. Therein lies one of the key elements of success: doing your absolute best at everything you do. For the champion, this means going the extra mile. Champions don't settle for mediocrity; they possess a spirit of excellence in all they do. The text says "whatever" because the principles are applicable to any number of contexts. In other words, some of these biblical teachings are going to help you be a success in your career, others in ministry, some in relationships, others in personal growth, etc.

Success, therefore, is directly related to whether or not you have put in your *best* effort—in every area of endeavor. You know when you've only done just enough to get by, and when you've really given it your all. Take for example a child who comes home with a *B* on a test at school. That's a good grade; it's above average. In most schools, a *B* puts you on the honor roll. However, if that student really could have done better but just didn't give it his all, then earning a *B* was not a success. There may be another student who brought home a *C*, and if that truly was the absolute best that student could do in that particular class, then that *C* represented a success. So comparatively, the *C* for the child who had done her best makes her more of a success than the *B* for the one who didn't try his best and could have done better.

The key principle is that when you keep God first in every way, He will then direct your efforts toward success…

Trust in the Lord with all thine heart; and lean not unto thine own understanding. In all thy ways acknowledge him, and He shall direct thy paths (Proverbs 3:5-6).

As you keep God first, as you acknowledge Him in all your ways, then whatever you choose to do with your hands will only be a choice that He has directed you to choose—which means that it can't fail.

Through faith and prayer, champions give the decision to God as to what their hands will do. Therefore, whatever the champion's hands find to do will only be that which came about as a revelation by God. In other words, keep God first, and He'll keep you on a successful path.

True champions receive their commands from God.

—*The Art of War*, VII.1 (paraphrased); Sun Tzu

CHAMPIONS RISK FAILURE

They went through the region of Phrygia and Galatia, having been forbidden by the Holy Spirit to speak the word in Asia. When they had come opposite Mysia, they attempted to go into Bithynia, but the Spirit of Jesus did not allow them; so, passing by Mysia, they went down to Troas. During the night Paul had a vision: there stood a man of Macedonia pleading with him and saying, "Come over to Macedonia and help us." When he had seen the vision, we immediately tried to cross over to Macedonia, being convinced that God had called us to proclaim the good news to them. We set sail from Troas and took a straight course to Samothrace, the following day to Neapolis, and from there to Philippi, which is a leading city of the district of Macedonia and a Roman colony. We remained in this city for some days (Acts 16:6-12 NRSV).

One of the ways that God leads and directs our hand to make a choice is by opening and closing doors of opportunity. In Acts 16 for example, Paul and his companions traveled throughout the region of Phrygia and Galatia after they were kept by the Holy Spirit from preaching the Word in the province of Asia. The implication was that it wasn't God's plan for them to preach in Asia. Then Paul says that when they got to the border of Mysia, they tried to enter Bithynia to preach, but the Spirit would not allow them there either. So they passed by Mysia and went down to Troas. During the night while Paul slept, he had a vision of a man from Macedonia begging him to come there and help them. So Paul concluded that the Lord had called them to preach the gospel in Macedonia, and they went immediately to preach in Philippi, the main city of Macedonia. (See Acts 16:6-10.)

Here's the point: You cannot be a success if you're not willing to risk failing. Paul and his companions tried this. They tried that. They tried the other. None of it worked, but they didn't force it, and they didn't quit. They simply trusted God. Then they heard Him in the night as they slept, and did as the Spirit directed them to do.

Champions learn to handle a "no" from God, because champions know that a closed door leads to a better open one. Like Paul, you keep knocking on doors until the right one opens.

"Success is going from one failure to another without losing your enthusiasm."

—Winston Churchill

Champions know how to handle losing. They don't allow a loss to demoralize them or convince them to quit. They learn from their failure so they can win the next time. Too many Christians are stuck in neutral because they are afraid to try. Many more are stuck because they're afraid to fail. There are also those who are afraid to try because they're afraid to *succeed*, because success brings with it additional responsibility (according to Luke 12:48b).

I know a woman who worked for a bank and who intentionally rejected two different job promotion offers. Her reason was that she didn't want to work that hard. To her, the extra effort wasn't worth the additional perks. What sets champions apart from average persons is that champions *want* to succeed. They are in the race to achieve the gold. Yet, champions are not afraid of failing, because champions are aware of a key reality: they know that if they fail, they are *not considered a failure*, because for champions, failure is never final.

> *A man plans his course, but the Lord determines his steps* (Proverbs 16:9 NIV).

Success is the result of God directing you. One of the ways He does that is by opening and closing doors. Paul stayed on the road until he hit a red light. Until God closed a door, Paul progressed along the path he started on.

Sometimes you may sense the Lord leading you to do something. Initiate your response to His calling by stepping through the door of opportunity that exists. Stay on the road until you hit a red light. Sometimes you will hit a green light. Sometimes you'll hit a yellow light. Sometimes you'll get a detour. But until the road ends or the door closes, stay on the course that God directs.

Paul's willingness to try different avenues in search of God's direction for his ministry serves as an example to champions today. When one way didn't work, Paul tried another. At first, it may have seemed that every closed door was an obstacle to God's plan, but it was actually an instrument of God to guide Paul where the Lord wanted him to be, and to be there in the Lord's timing.

GOD'S PROVIDENCE

There is a providential dimension to success. In other words, there are things that you have been exposed to and learned and experienced along the path of your life, things that perhaps you've even forgotten or that you thought at the time had little or no value to you. But those things comprise the individual cobblestones of your pathway to success. God takes your experiences from one, five, ten years ago, and uses them to forge and shape and mold you into the champion He wants you to be. That's why champions are always willing to trust God to lead them. They know that success is a result of God directing their path.

In all thy ways acknowledge him, and he shall direct thy paths (Proverbs 3:6).

The great thing about the lesson of Acts 16 is that it teaches about a guy who was willing to try and try and try until finally he got a clear revelation from God as to precisely what he was to do. And I have no doubt that somewhere along the way in his ceaseless efforts, Paul probably learned some things that were going to help him when he arrived where God directed him.

THE DESIRES OF YOUR HEART

Trust in the Lord, and do good; so shalt thou dwell in the land, and verily thou shalt be fed. Delight thyself also in the Lord; and he shall give thee the desires of thine heart (Psalm 37:3-4).

This Scripture is often misunderstood (see Ps. 37:3-4). "The desires of thine heart" does not mean that God is your celestial genie waiting to fulfill your every desire. He is not a cosmic wishing well. In fact, I can attest that I'm glad He didn't give me some of the things I've wanted during my life. All you have to do is look at your past boyfriend or girlfriend and realize that you didn't always seek the best desires for yourself! Many people have gotten what they desired, only to want to trade it in after feeling buyer's remorse later on.

To trust in the Lord and He will "give" you the desires of your heart does not mean *give* in the sense of "fulfill." It means *give* in the sense of "deposit." It's the idea of putting something in place, like putting a ring on a finger or a helmet on your head. So the text can be more properly translated as, "Trust in the Lord and He will deposit within your heart certain desires." When you put God first, when you rely upon God, when you put your trust and faith fully in Him, the result is that He deposits into your heart the desires that He wants you to desire, which then become your desires.

Putting it all together, when you put God first, and in all your ways acknowledge Him (see Prov. 3:6), and you do with all your might what your hands find to do (see Eccles. 9:10), then your hands will only find those things that God directs you to do, on the path that He drives you onto, because in putting Him first, you have invited Him to deposit into your heart His desire, which then becomes your desire (see Ps. 37:4).

Here is the practical flow of Proverbs 3:6, Ecclesiastes 9:10, and Psalm 37:4...

When:

I acknowledge and obey God

and:

I find work to perform

and:

I delight myself in the Lord

Then:

God deposits desires into my heart

and:

God brings to fruition the desires of my heart

It's all about surrendering to God's desire that you be productive, successful, and of use in His Kingdom.

THE VISION FOR YOUR CHAMPIONSHIP

Then the Lord answered me and said: "Write the vision and make it plain on tablets, that he may run who reads it. For the vision is yet for an appointed time; but at the end it will speak, and it will not lie. Though it tarries, wait for it; because it will surely come, it will not tarry (Habakkuk 2:2-3 NKJV).

In the passage above, the prophet Habakkuk gives a three-step sequence that is crucial to drawing out the champion in you. Let's look at the chronology:

FIRST: WRITE THE VISION

Habakkuk 2:2 says to write the vision plainly on tablets. In today's culture that would be translated as, "Put it up on a billboard." Once you have a vision, write it clearly, because you will never be a champion if you cannot envision yourself as one.

"Write the vision" is akin to "you must be able to visualize your success." Have a picture in your mind of what success looks like in whatever area you're working. If it's your career, you ought to have a picture in your mind of what it will look like five or ten years down the road in that career. You may not be there now, but you can see yourself there in your thoughts, and as God directs your path, it becomes clear in your mind.

SECOND: SO THOSE WHO RUN WILL SEE IT

The next step comes in the phrase "that he may run who reads it." There are two aspects to the idea of "run." First, *run* means that it's written so plainly that a person running past it doesn't even have to stop to be able to read it. It's so clear and concise that they can understand it even as they rush by.

Second, it means that the vision is so clear that not only the person running past can get it, but that a person can quickly grasp the vision in his or her mind and then tell someone else who hasn't even seen it, and that individual will get the revelation too.

THIRD: WRITE THE VISION *IN PENCIL*

The final step in the Habakkuk process is to write the vision in pencil, because your own life should tell you: *things change*. And champions are prepared to adjust.

When we sat down and wrestled through the vision for Faithful Central Bible Church, we found that we were constantly tweaking and updating and revising the plan. We prayed over it and clarified it and adjusted it, in order to have a clear sense of a direction of where we were going and where God was leading us for the next three, five, and ten years. We wrote what we could in accordance with how far we could see down the road at that time.

Then we decided to carry the vision one step further and go to a place we were envisioning as our future home. So we rented the Great Western Forum sports arena in Los Angeles, and we brought in film cameras and produced a video about the history of Faithful Central Bible Church. We brought our congregation in, too, so they could get a visual picture of the vision as we explained it to them.

Then an unexpected thing happened. When we were all together in the arena, we began to feel pretty good—we could get used to that place! It was after that that we adjusted our vision to actually purchase the Forum, former home of the Los Angeles Lakers pro basketball team.

We had a plan. We had a vision. We had a direction. If we had not written the vision down, we would have never gotten on the road toward *something*. And we wrote it down in pencil, which allowed us to adjust our original plan and detour to a much better plan.

In order to be a success, champions have the vision and the direction, but they write it in pencil, because whatever we plan is always subject to possible overrule by God.

He who exercises no forethought is sure to be defeated.

—*The Art of War*, IX.41 (paraphrased); Sun Tzu

Many people miss the mark because they wait around for God to give them the final revelation. They spend precious time doing little or nothing, because they don't want to start something that might not be their ultimate and final destination. But what they don't realize is that if they don't take the first bus part of the way, they'll never catch the next bus that leads the rest of the way to the destination.

To visualize your plan but write it in pencil means to not be stagnant, to keep the ball moving forward, to get the team down-field toward the goal line. You never know what next step will lead to that unexpected great play.

A few years ago I was scheduled to speak at a Promise Keepers meeting of nearly 75,000 men. As I took the stage, my knees literally got weak. I was overwhelmed because I had never even seen 75,000 people gathered in one place before (the seating capacity of Faithful Central Bible Church is only 17,500).

After the meeting, probably two dozen different reporters asked me, "Did you ever think it would be this big?"

My answer was the same to every one of them: "I always knew it would be big. I just didn't know it would be *this* big." Because every time I thought I had seen what big was, God always said, "No...it's *bigger* than that."

You may not have the fine details of your vision quite set yet, but write down, document, notate, and focus on the part that you *do* have. If you are keeping God first in every area of your life, then you can be confident in trusting that if there is more to the vision, He will deliver it to you. In the meantime, until you hit a red light, stay on that road with a faithful assumption that it is of God.

HABAKKUK'S BURDEN

Most people miss the sequence of vision revelation. The often cited and quoted classic verse on vision is Habakkuk 2:2, which speaks about writing the vision. But careful examination of the text and the context will reveal that the vision of Habakkuk 2:2 does not begin in Habakkuk 2:2. In fact, the vision of Habakkuk 2:2 begins with his burden of Habakkuk 1:1. The foundation of Habakkuk's process was a particular burden that he was under, which caused him to take his lament to the Lord. (See Hab. 2:2; 1:1.) The lesson is that any vision you receive will be related to a revelation, but will not *begin* with that revelation. God isn't prone to simply plopping something into your life. He doesn't usually just suddenly toss a vision or a plan your way. Visions are always matched up with, and preceded by, a specific burden.

Let's examine the lament stirring around in Habakkuk, which he took to God and that ultimately launched the vision:

The burden which the prophet Habakkuk saw. O Lord, how long shall I cry, and You will not hear? Even cry out to You, "Violence!" and You will not save. Why do You show me iniquity, and cause me to see trouble? For plundering and violence are before me; there is strife, and contention arises. Therefore the law is powerless, and justice never goes forth. For the wicked surround the righteous; therefore perverse judgment proceeds (Habakkuk 1:1-4 NKJV).

Before Habakkuk got his vision in chapter 2, he had been experiencing a burden, which he had taken to God in chapter 1. Habakkuk had a passion and a burden for the people. "How long, Lord," he cried out in chapter one, "how long must your people cry out? How long?" He had a heart for the people; and his burden was that they were wallowing in blatant sin (see Hab. 1:1-4).

God does not mismatch burdens and visions. He always connects vision with burden—but it starts with burden. God deposits into your heart a burden. From that burden, God gives revelation, vision, as to how that burden will be fleshed out in your life. For example, God probably won't call you to do something that you hate. Nor is He likely to call you to do something you are not equipped to do. He equips us and gives us what we need to fulfill His vision for us, which is launched from our burden.

For instance, God probably will not call you to play violin with the philharmonic if you can't tell the difference between a violin and a viola. That anointing will most likely not suddenly come over you one morning with God calling you to quit your job as a rancher and go play at the Met that evening. Believe me, God will not call you and assign you to be a violinist if you cannot do the job. For you, playing violin would not be God's definition of making a joyful noise. Make your joyful noise on an old fiddle down in the basement. Make a joyful noise playing air violin over at the karaoke restaurant on a Friday night. But don't get up onstage and draw a bow across those strings if it'll ruin eardrums.

If you don't have the burden, if you don't have the desire, if you don't have the ability, if you don't have the wherewithal or the education or training to do what you think God has called you to do, then God is not the one calling you to do it. It might be your mom calling you, or your fiancée, or yourself, but it's not God.

It is also a mistake to measure the veracity of a burden based solely on how much money can be made. Vision and career choices are made based on passion and burden, not on income. For example, if you really enjoy working with people and helping people work through their problems, but you don't really care for computers, then

God is not likely to call you to be a computer technician. The problem arises, however, when you discover that computer techs make more money than counselors. If you're attracted to a bigger paycheck and you set aside your passion for helping people and counseling, and pursue a computer science degree and maybe even pass the test, but you're not functioning under your love for people, then at some point it will be revealed that you are bored to tears. Locked up in a cubicle at a computer keyboard you will find yourself about to climb the walls, wishing you were spending your time interacting with people and their challenges. The bottom line is that you are only doing it to get a big paycheck. You will make a good living but you won't be making such a good life.

Many people miss their calling because they resist the doors God has opened for them to step into their burden and passion. It all begins with a burden. God gives the ability to match the burden. Sometimes that ability is progressive. For example, God may have called you to be an attorney; so you start that journey by going to law school.

I was once approached by a young lady who wanted a career in computer science. Yet, she told me she hated math, hated algebra, hated numbers—she hated pretty much everything that had to do with computing.

"You say your call in life is to do work with computers," I said to her, "yet you don't like working with numbers. Is that right?"

"That's right," she responded.

"And you hate math too, correct?"

"Yes," she nodded.

"Then listen to me," I said. "This is very important: you've looked at two different schools that offer degrees in this area, and both curricula include several courses in math. Obviously, math is required, because those skills are crucial to working with computers. Either you are going to have to dig in and learn math, or you might want to consider another vocation."

When God places a vision in champions, nothing will stand in their way to prevent them from seeing that vision through to reality, because they allow God to lead them to its fulfillment.

When the great champion Joshua received his vision from God, this is what God told him:

> *I will give you every place where you set your foot, as I promised Moses....No one will be able to stand up against you all the days of your life. As I was with Moses, so I will be with you; I will never leave you nor forsake you....Be strong and very courageous. Be careful to obey all the law my servant Moses gave you; do not turn from it to the right or to the left, that you may be successful wherever you go. Do not let this Book of the Law depart from your mouth; meditate on it day and night, so that you may be careful to do everything written in it. Then you will be prosperous and successful. Have I not commanded you? Be strong and courageous. Do not be terrified; do not be discouraged, for the LORD your God will be with you wherever you go* (Joshua 1:3,5,7-9 NIV).

"No one will be able to stand up against you" and "you will be prosperous and successful" means this (Josh. 1:5,8): if God has called you to go to the ends of this earth, I don't care who gets in your way, you'll go. If you have to step over people trying to block you, if you have to go around them, if you have to go under them, God will give you what it takes to do so. And you will have the mindset to go through whatever you have to go through, because that's a part of being a champion in God.

If the burden comes from God, and math is a requirement or a stepping stone to achieving the vision, then even if you don't like math, He will give you the ability and the internal peace to handle it and to get through it.

THE CHAMPION'S MOTIVE: ALL TO THE GLORY OF GOD

Whether therefore ye eat, or drink, or whatsoever ye do, do all to the glory of God (1 Corinthians 10:31).

Here is the most important key you will ever receive about walking in success: the goal of champions is to do all they can to glorify God, and to glorify God in all they do. If what you have chosen to do does not bring honor and glory to God, then it does not matter how well you do it, you will not become a champion at it.

But what does "glorify God" mean? This is one of our "Christianese" terms (you know, one of those phrases that everybody in church uses, and if you don't go to church you really don't know what it means—in fact some of those who use it don't really understand what it means). How do we glorify God? Glory has to do with a light or a radiating illumination that shines forth an image. To glorify God means this: to leave an accurate portrait, image, or impression of God that gives Him His righteous due.

The seventeenth chapter of the book of John is rightly called the "Lord's Prayer." However, many people believe that the Lord's Prayer is the one Jesus gave to believers as our model prayer, which begins, "Our Father which art in heaven, hallowed be thy name" (see Matt. 6). But that is not the "Lord's Prayer." It is an example that the Lord gave to the disciples of *how* we are to pray. Jesus would never pray the Matthew 6 prayer, because He was sinless and didn't need forgiveness. But He did pray the John 17 prayer, which is actually known as the "High Priestly Prayer." (See John 17.)

As Jesus began the prayer, He told us something that is found nowhere else in all of Scripture. Most of us have used the phrases, "Glorify God," "Bring glory to God," or "Give God the glory." But only in Jesus' High Priestly Prayer can we glean information that will help us to understand what it means to truly glorify God. Notice what Jesus prayed as He began to speak:

*Jesus spoke these words, lifted up His eyes to heaven, and said: "Father, the hour has come. Glorify Your Son, that Your Son also may glorify You, as You have given Him authority over all flesh, that He should give eternal life to as many as You have given Him. And this is eternal life, that they may know You, the only true God, and Jesus Christ whom You have sent. **I have glorified You on the earth. I have finished the work which You have given Me to do**"* (John 17:1-4 NKJV).

The first revelation of the text is that whatever *glorifying God* means, Jesus did it. He says, *I glorified the Father* (see John 17:4).

But notice that He goes on to give a description—and I might say, a *definition*—of what it means to glorify God. He says in verse four, "I have finished the work which You have given me to do" (John 17:4 NKJV). There it is! Jesus glorified God by finishing the work that God told Him to do. Thus, the revelation is clear: we glorify God only by *doing the assignment He has given us to do.*

Every version of the Bible connects glorifying God with doing what He tells us to do. The *New International Version* of the Bible uses the phrase, "I have brought you glory on earth by completing the work you gave me to do." The *New Revised Standard Version* says, "I glorified you on earth by finishing the work that you gave me to do." *The Living Bible* puts it this way: "I brought glory to you here on earth by doing everything you told me to." The *New American Standard Bible* says, "I glorified You on the earth, having accomplished the work which You have given Me to do." (See John 17:4 NIV, NRSV, TLB, NASB.)

You have been assigned to honor and obey God in all you do. That is how to glorify Him. You have an assignment, a destiny, a call on your life, and you glorify God by doing just that—fulfilling His call and destiny upon your life.

When I was a student at the University of Illinois, I was enrolled in a class that I got into the habit of cutting constantly. I think it was a class in criminology; and I think I took this class because some classmates of mine said it was an easy *A* (yeah, right!). I don't recall how often I was actually in the class, because I was so busy cutting it that I lost track. The class syllabus stated that we only earned two grades: a midterm grade and a final grade. The midterm was a paper. Since I had cut the class so often, I came up with the bright idea to use the syllabus as a guide to write my midterm. I waited until the last possible minute to write that paper, and I spent the last couple of days in the library getting it finished—and we didn't have computers back in those days; I did it all in longhand.

I turned in the paper, smug that I'd beaten the system and saved myself weeks of effort. When I got my paper back a week later, the professor had scribbled notes all over it (when there are little handwritten notes all over your midterm paper, that's your first clue that things aren't going well). The professor's note said, "Great paper. Good research. Great content. Grade 'F'"—and the *F* was in red ink and had a circle around it! There was a note at the bottom of the paper that said, "You received an F, Mister Ulmer, because this was not the assignment."

There are some people who will miss Heaven because they did not do what they were assigned to do, but instead took some ill-informed "shortcut" that led completely away from God. Here's what the Bible says about shortcuts:

Many will say to Me in that day, "Lord, Lord, have we not prophesied in Your name, cast out demons in Your name, and done many wonders in Your name?" And then I will declare to them, "I never knew you; depart from Me, you who practice lawlessness!" (Matthew 7:22-23 NKJV)

The most important part of being a champion is rightly representing God. If what you are doing in your life brings glory and honor to God, then you are being the person God created you to be.

"If you are not actively pursuing the person you want to be, then you are pursuing the person you don't want to be." — Theodore Roosevelt

THE CHAMPION'S VISION: ANCHORED IN FAITH

But without faith it is impossible to please Him: for he that cometh to God must believe that He is, and that He is a rewarder of them that diligently seek Him (Hebrews 11:6).

Being a champion in the Lord means choosing by faith God's destiny and design for your life and fulfilling it with maximum effort by relying upon the power of the Holy Spirit. God will not force you to be a champion. You choose to be one by placing faith in His plan for you.

Several years ago our ministry designed a 5,000-seat sanctuary by faith. It was going to cost us several million dollars for those 5,000-seats. We stayed on the path of that new 5,000-seat sanctuary until we got to a fork in the road and God revealed to us that He had better plans for the use of His money. His revelation: why pay that many millions for 5,000 seats when we could pay just 20 percent more to purchase the Great Western Forum and have nearly a 250 percent higher seating capacity *and* own a venue that is used more than a couple of times per week for a few hours?

So by faith, we purchased The Forum. And by faith it became a vehicle for the expansion of the philosophy of our ministry, which is not something that is only carried on behind stained glass windows and closed doors and padded pews once or twice per week, but is done out in the fabric, in the essence, and the very core of the community. We do that by providing jobs, services, and entertainment—as an extension of our ministry. That purchase was a far wiser use of God's resources than building a much smaller venue that we would have used two or three times per week and that would have remained mostly unused the rest of the time.

Over the years, since we purchased the Forum, I've had many people ask me, "What's your secret? What's the attraction? How do you get that many thousands of people to come to church at the Forum?"

I tell them all the same thing: "There is nothing that we do that someone else is not doing. We're not the only church in town that has a good music ministry. We're not the only church in town where the teaching of the Word of God is going forth clearly and powerfully. I can't give you a quick answer or some formula. We are just a people who had enough faith to believe we could occupy the Forum with people who glorify God. *He* did it. That's it."

It does not sit well with the world when you give all the glory to God. But it's not about us. It's about Him. We are champions who understand that our success is anchored in pursuing the burden God gave us and in focusing all of the glory on Him during that journey.

BE *GOD'S* BEST

Recently a television special aired about eighth or ninth-grade children with learning disabilities who had taken a test. The kids could only read at a fourth-grade level, yet they had gotten all of the answers correct. The excitement and the joy on their faces was remarkable. They were champions simply because they had done their best.

My daddy often used to say something to me that I had always laughed at, until I got older and finally understood what he meant. He said, "Son, be the best *whatever* that you choose to be. If you are going to be a garbage collector, then get an award for being the best garbage collector on the route."

"That's a funny little thing to tell your son," I responded. But one day it dawned on me that all he'd been trying to tell me was that God did not make me to be a failure, and that if I would just do my best at what He gave me to do, then in God's eyes I was a champion and therefore a success.

The fulfillment of the champion's passion brings glory to God. Whatever your burden is, if you will do it to the absolute best of your ability, then success will follow. It could be your career. It could be your relationship with your husband or wife. It could be your health. It could be your peace of mind. It could be a financial goal. It could be helping people who are dealing with struggles you've been trained to alleviate. It could be in being a better parent or grandparent.

Becoming a champion starts with a burden within you, a passion that you have taken to God. *Follow that passion* to wherever God leads you, give all glory to Him, and you will become a champion who understands success.

ENDNOTE

1. Webster's Dictionary, 11th ed. s.v. "success."

Chapter 9

Champions Deal With Success

"Those who know how to win are much more numerous than those who know how to make proper use of their victories."

—History; Polybius (c. 203-120 B.C.)

A close friend of mine was probably one of the most gifted pastors, preachers, and evangelists I've ever known. He started in a little church out in the country. From that little church he moved to another church, relatively close to a large metropolitan area, and that church grew even larger than his first one. At that time, it was the largest church building I had ever been in. The place would seat 6,000. One visit to that church and you would never forget it. To get there, you would leave the big city and drive out to the middle of nowhere, and the highway would take a dip, and you'd come up out of a shallow little valley, and suddenly that church would loom big as a mountain in front of you.

Around that time, the church services were televised nationally and internationally. My friend, the pastor, was in great demand all around the world. He had all of the perks and accoutrements of success. Money, clothes, cars, plane, you name it. He was in demand literally around the world. He was dubbed by some as the next Billy Graham. Thousands would come to hear him minister.

One day I was in a meeting with a very wise friend and spiritual father figure to me, a man who speaks into my life. He said to me, "We need to pray for John [not his real name]," referring to this pastor and his big church out in the country. Surprised, I asked why. He responded, "Because if he does not turn, if he does not change the path he is on, within one year he is going to fall."

At that time, nothing was happening either visibly or publicly that any of us were aware of. But this prophet was a very wise man, and almost like clockwork, eleven months after this sage spoke those words to me, the pastor fell. The wise prophet then added words about that fallen pastor that I will never forget. He said, "[John] has surrounded himself with people who mean him no good."

He did not fall morally. He did not fall sexually. He did not get caught in some torrid affair with a coworker or anything like that. I see it so clearly now in hindsight because of the prophetic word spoken by the wise prophet. But here is what's scary: it was from the ministry and message of this brother who fell that I heard a warning that also has stuck with me. In a message, John himself preached about the two continual challenges a pastor faces (which I have shared around the world with young and not-so-young pastors). John said that pastors struggle with "the intoxication of success, or the devastation of insignificance." Looking back on his life and ministry, I now see that it was as if he were prophesying to himself and warning himself.

The pastor fell because he was intoxicated with success. The man had become almost drunk with his achievements. He could not handle it. Apparently this pastor had hired some media people and publicists who promised him they would "make him a star." He was so obsessed with being a success that he had placed his destiny and his ministry and his reputation in the hands of those who had promised to lay the world at his feet.

The intoxication of success will entice you to be a champion at *any* cost—the cost of your integrity, the cost of your family, the cost of your testimony, the cost of your relationship with your children, the cost of the very victory you seek. Because of the intoxication of success, your gifts will often take you where your character cannot keep you. You will stand operating more out of the ability to exercise your giftedness than the anointing of the Spirit who gives you the gifts.

Many Christians will taste significant success as champions in their chosen fields of endeavor. Many are already there. Success for the champion means fulfilling God's destiny and desire. It means having the empowerment of the Spirit of God. It is crucial that you handle your success better than my friend did...because even champions can fall.

CAN GOD TRUST YOU WITH SUCCESS?

If not careful, even a champion can be lured into the intoxication of success. My pastor friend, John, was a champion until he allowed himself to be mesmerized by fame and fortune. If a champion isn't vigilant, he can become so obsessed with succeeding that he can actually put blinders on and run the risk of missing God. What is even more tragic is when you have tasted success and know it personally, but then lose it because you didn't handle it correctly.

Dr. David Hocking, a former professor and academic mentor of mine, taught me that believers are under constant assault from three mortal enemies:

The flesh.

The devil.

The world.

These are their goals:

It is the goal of the flesh to give you pleasure without God.

It is the goal of satan to make you religious without God.

It is the goal of the world to make you successful without God.

The starting point for the champion to vanquish the assaults from these enemies is, as always, the Word of God...

You say in your heart, "My power and the might of my hand have gained me this wealth." And you shall remember the Lord your God, for it is He who gives you power to get wealth, that He may establish His covenant which He swore to your fathers, as it is this day (Deuteronomy 8:17-18 NKJV).

Both riches and honor come from You, and You reign over all. In Your hand is power and might; in Your hand it is to make great and to give strength to all (1 Chronicles 29:12 NKJV).

I'm not going to spend a lot of time here examining the topics of money and wealth,[1] but let's look at the topic as it relates to the success of a champion. As God says in the passages above, it is He who gives us the power to gain wealth, and He is the source of all riches and honor. For this discussion only, I will describe *wealth* as one of the synonyms I use for "success," because there are people who would measure success by one's wealth or material gain (please know that *I* do *not* ascribe to such a narrow definition of success!).

Don't ever feel like money itself is bad or evil. It's not. Money is not a sin. Money is not "the root of all evil"—it is the *love of money* that becomes the root, the cause of sinful actions (see 1 Tim. 6:10). At the other extreme, don't adopt a position that deifies or sanctifies poverty, either. There are people who espouse a pseudo-spiritual argument that denounces and diminishes the importance of money (this is an unbiblical point of view). It is the desire to accumulate or hoard money that becomes the seedbed and root for evil thoughts and actions, and which can snare the champion.

The ability to get wealth, the ability to be successful, comes from God alone. It is part of His covenant, which is a covenant of blessing. Remember, wealth is relative. For some people, for example, paying their bills on time (versus always paying late) represents an experiencing of a certain level of success in handling wealth.

Many people need to reprogram their minds and press the *delete* button over what they've learned about money. Too often, Christians are taught that it is more spiritual to be poor. Others have been taught just the opposite, that the essence of spirituality is measured financially or in terms of material gain. However, this generation labors under the delusion of a negative spin on the reality of money and its place in God's economy on earth. If God is the

One who gives the ability to gain it or to get it, then money in itself cannot be bad. However, there is a caveat attached to God allowing us material possessions:

> *If you by any means forget the Lord your God, and follow other gods, and serve them and worship them, I testify against you this day that you shall surely perish* (Deuteronomy 8:19 NKJV).

It is urgent that the champion understand that the same God who allows you to be successful is also God enough to take that success away from you if you veer off of His path.

An arrogant spirit has crept into the Body of Christ to the point where (as Dr. Jack Hayford puts it) the rules don't count anymore. Some feel validated by their success, and they take the attitude that it is theirs permanently, as if nothing and nobody will take it away from them. They take the position that it is the devil who wants to take it away from them, when in fact the text makes it clear that God can and will remove success from us if we don't handle it His way. As the Scripture above warns, unrepentant disobedience can eliminate blessings. Worse than that, it can invite disaster into the life of a champion.

It is the Lord who positions you for greatness. It is God who gives riches and honor. It is He who makes you a champion and gives you success. He does all of this as a *trust*. The question is not whether you can be a success. The real question is, can God trust you to handle success when you get it? When you achieve whatever destiny God set for you, can you manage it His way? Will you treat people properly? Will you behave differently toward others? How are you going to respond to those you used to know on your way up? How are you going to relate to people who don't yet have your level of success? Who are you going to treat differently just because they don't have what you have?

That pastor friend of mine who did not handle success well had allowed himself to become intoxicated with it. He acquired an arrogant boastfulness about the blessings God bestowed upon him.

Success is from the hand of God, and He can easily take it away from you if you don't live your life in accordance with His will and His ways.

> *I warned the **proud** to cease their arrogance! I told the wicked to lower their **insolent gaze** and to stop being **stubborn and proud**. For promotion and power come from nowhere on earth, but only from God. He promotes one and deposes another* (Psalm 75:4-6 TLB).

No Shortcuts

The Bible teaches that success comes from God. God has the power to lift a person up. God has the power to bring a person down. Now look at the spin the devil puts on success and possessions:

> *Again, the devil taketh him up into an exceeding high mountain, and sheweth him all the kingdoms of the world, and the glory of them; and saith unto him, All these things will I give thee, if thou wilt fall down and worship me* (Matthew 4:8-9).

The devil offered—to the One who is already King—kingship over all the kingdoms of the world! When the devil tries to cut a deal with you, he says, "Look. If you will bow down before me, I will give you worldly success, I'll give you wealth, I will give you position and power. All you gotta do is just bow before me."

The word *bow* is used in the context of "worship." The devil was saying that he would give Jesus the kingdoms of the world, that he would make Him a world success, but without God. Satan's scam was that he would give Jesus *what He was already destined to have anyway*, but with one twist: Jesus would have the fulfillment of His destiny, but by a shortcut—bypassing Calvary (which would have short circuited God's entire redemptive plan of salvation).

There is another interesting revelation in this text. The deal satan tries to cut with Jesus is this: I will give you all of this if you will just bow down. As I said, *bow* means "to fall down in worship."[2] But there is something else. This word for "bow" is in the aorist tense. This tense is used to express an action at a specific point in time; an action *in the moment*. So, in effect, here is what the devil is saying to Jesus: "I will give you all of this if you will bow and worship me in this moment of time, if you will bow down right now, just this one time, I will give you all the kingdoms of the world." Remember, they are in the desert, the wilderness. There is no one there but Jesus and the devil. The enemy is saying, "Now come on, Jesus. No one is here. No one is watching. If you won't tell, I won't tell. Come on, bow just this one time and it's all yours." It will only cost you one bow!

Does this scenario sound familiar to you? Ever felt like you could bow just once and get away with it? Ever heard the enemy whispering in your ear, "Aww, come on. One time won't hurt."

Remember, Eve and Adam only ate the forbidden fruit *one time!* David only slept with Bathsheba *one time.*

What's your price? What can be offered to you to make you compromise your integrity and lose your destiny just for the sake of success? Here is the devil's deal: he will give you what you want, he will help you fulfill your purpose, and you will bow down and worship him. And then you will pay for it.

Champions do not put a price on their integrity and testimony. They compromise nothing. They're not interested in success at any cost. They're only interested in success *God's way.*

Be careful when you're looking for a shortcut. You cannot microwave maturity. I am amazed when people come into Faithful Central Bible Church with the strange notion that it all sprang up overnight. They say, "Wow! How did you get all this so fast?" They don't know a thing about my wife and me starting with a church of three people more than a quarter of a century ago. We took no shortcut.

CHAMPIONS DON'T MISHANDLE SUCCESS

The context of the passage below refers to people who have mishandled their success. It talks about those who have received wealth and attained power and prestige; and yet they have mishandled it. The suggestion is that their riches did them no good...

Come now, you rich, weep and howl for your miseries that are coming upon you! Your riches are corrupted, and your garments are moth-eaten. Your gold and silver are corroded, and their corrosion will be a witness against you and will eat your flesh like fire. You have heaped up treasure in the last days. Indeed the wages of the laborers who mowed your fields, which you kept back by fraud, cry out; and the cries of the reapers have reached the ears of the Lord of Sabaoth. You have lived on the earth in pleasure and luxury; you have fattened your hearts as in a day of slaughter. You have condemned, you have murdered the just; he does not resist you (James 5:1-6 NKJV).

Some people want to have a lot more money in their bank account, but they aren't spiritually rich enough in their mindset to properly handle any more. The goal is to gain the ability to first handle what you have. Verse four says that the cries of the field workers who have been cheated of their pay have reached the ears of the Lord, which is an indication that God cares about social and economic injustice and inequity (see James 5:4).

For most people, success will be defined in some sense through the context of a career. For most, that career will necessitate that they have some interaction with somebody. For example, if you are climbing the corporate ladder, at some point you will go from the bottom of the ladder to moving up the ladder. You will have people above you and you will have people who are subordinate to you. In terms of being successful in your career, it is important to learn how to relate to those who report to you.

James 5:4 talks about people who are in a position of authority and have achieved success but have cheated those who worked under them (see James 5:4). They were so obsessed and concerned with their own well-being that they had no sensitivity or compassion for those who worked for them.

If you're a Christian and you have workers reporting to you, you should be setting the example of how to treat subordinates; you should be looked to by your unsaved fellow managers as the pattern to follow. Champions stand out as different. If your walk with God can't impact your walk in life on that level, then you're not where God wants you to be in your walk with Him. If your walk with Christ does not impact how you interact with people every day at work, then you're not where a champion needs to be.

Champions don't lie in order to get ahead. They don't pass on vicious rumors at the coffee shop. They don't carelessly damage reputations. The Word of God is not the standard for unbelievers; His standard and authority are over us who claim the name of Christ. It may buck the principles of today's culture, but champions are to rise as examples in touching, encouraging, and uplifting others, in leading those who work for them, and in following those they report to. God is not as impressed with how you deal with people at your church on Sunday morning, or whether you speak in tongues and dance up and down the aisles, as He is about how you treat people out in the world.

You have lived on earth in luxury and self-indulgence. You have fattened yourselves in the day of slaughter (James 5:5 NIV).

The Giver of Success

He who loves money shall never have enough. The foolishness of thinking that wealth brings happiness! The more you have, the more you spend, right up to the limits of your income, so what is the advantage of wealth—except perhaps to watch it as it runs through your fingers! (Ecclesiastes 5:10-11 TLB)

The text above was written nearly 3,000 years ago, yet it perfectly reflects societal attitudes today. We live in an age of such a consumerist theology that many Christians actually believe that God exists just to *give them stuff*. They think that it is the sole desire of God to make them happy. Everything revolves around *me*.

You earned it!

You deserve a break today!

Have it your way!

You deserve the best!

The focus is always on *self*, and the desire is to get it *now*.

If you are going to handle success in a manner that honors God, your focus is not to be on success. Your focus is to be on the Giver of success. Your focus is to be on your relationship with God. That means that as a champion you must recognize the strategy of the enemy, which is to pervert the calling that God has placed upon your life.

You can actually miss the God who desires to give you success by going after the success and not the God who gives it. The Bible warns that it is foolish to think that money will make us happy. The enemy wants to convince us that we cannot be happy without it. The way we handle success is to realize that success itself doesn't necessarily make one happy (people can be successful without God); it is living a life in the joy of the Lord that makes one happy.

In Ecclesiastes 5:11, Solomon states, "What is the advantage of wealth—except perhaps to watch it as it runs through your fingers!" (Eccles. 5:11 TLB). You may have watched money run through your fingers at one time or another in your life. Here today, gone tomorrow. Car today, bus tomorrow. How foolish it is to think that money can make us happy. When people are obsessed with money, then the more they have, the more they'll spend and the more they'll want. And, the Scripture says, they spend it right up to the limits of their income. Many people today are only one paycheck away from the unemployment line. Many have a decent income; they just don't know how to handle it properly.

Proverbs 13:22 says that a wise man leaves an inheritance for his children's children. Thus, the measure of success for champions is not seen when people look at them, nor at their children. The measure of the success of champions is seen in the behavior, beliefs, and lifestyle of their grandchildren, because God measures success *transgenerationally*, not financially.

CHAMPIONS DON'T COMPROMISE THEIR SUCCESS

When times are good, be happy; but when times are bad, consider: God has made the one as well as the other. Therefore, a man cannot discover anything about his future (Ecclesiastes 7:14 NIV).

There's no greater area that will test your integrity, your character, your relationship with God, your faithfulness to God, than how you handle success. Your attitude toward success, financial blessing, money, and prosperity, and how you handle them, reveals your very character.

Genesis 22:1 says, "God tested Abraham" (Gen. 22:1 NKJV). Here was the test: was Abraham willing to give up his prized possession—his only son—to hold on to God? What are you willing to let go of (as lucrative as it may appear) if having it will make you compromise who you are as an ambassador of Christ? Is there any success you would give up related to your husband if such success were to cause you to stumble in your walk with the Lord? If you work twelve hours a day and it erodes the love affair between you and your wife, at some point you've got to ask yourself if it's worth it. As you work two jobs to support children you rarely get to spend quality time with, you are going to have to eventually ask, "Is this worth the price?" Where do you draw the line? Where do you separate success and compromise? Champions are willing to give up or to pass up anything that would compromise their walk with God.

Let's take a look at another great champion from history: Joseph, son of Jacob, grandson of Isaac, great-grandson of Abraham. The great story about Joseph spanned many years and taught many crucial lessons. He was the second youngest of the twelve sons of Jacob. He started out basically as a mama's boy who went on to become one of Israel's greatest champions.

We'll examine five of the lessons to be learned through Joseph that apply directly to becoming a champion:

1. **Listening**

2. **Planning**

3. **Managing**

4. **Providing**

5. **Blessing**

1: CHAMPIONS LISTEN

Genesis 41 tells the story about two troubling dreams that Pharaoh had while Joseph was in prison on false charges brought against him by the wife of Potiphar, captain of Pharaoh's palace guard. The dreams were so disturbing that Pharaoh summoned all of the magicians and wise men of the realm to listen to them and interpret them; but none could. Then the chief cupbearer remembered how Joseph had correctly interpreted dreams that he and the palace baker had two years earlier when they had been briefly imprisoned for offenses against Pharaoh. So Pharaoh summoned Joseph from the dungeon and asked him if he could interpret the king's dreams. (See Genesis 41:1-39.)

Two years earlier, when the baker and the cupbearer had asked Joseph to interpret their dreams while the three were in prison together, Joseph's response had been, "Do not interpretations belong to God? Tell me your dreams" (Gen. 40:8 NIV). In other words, before Joseph even listened to the dream, he gave glory to God (whom Joseph acknowledged would be the One doing the interpreting through him) and then he correctly interpreted the dreams.

Now it's two years after that incident. Pharaoh has Joseph brought up from the prison and asks him if he can interpret the disturbing dreams of the king. Joseph replies, "I cannot do it...but God will give Pharaoh the answer he desires" (Gen. 41:16 NIV). Thus, as he did with the cupbearer and baker two years earlier, Joseph first gave glory to God, then he listened to Pharaoh's dreams, and then he correctly gave the king God's interpretation of the dreams.

Joseph was so tuned in to God that he could listen to a dream and God would give him the correct interpretation of it. First, Joseph gave glory to Yahweh. Then he quietly, patiently listened to the dream. In other words, Joseph had learned to *listen* and to *hear*—to listen to and hear God, and to listen to and to hear others.

In Genesis 42, perhaps nine or ten years after Joseph interpreted Pharaoh's dreams and had been set by the king as second in command over all of Egypt, and a couple of years into the famine that had been ravaging the world, Joseph's brothers made their first journey to Egypt to request provisions to get them through the crisis. They went before Joseph—not knowing that this was their own young brother—and Joseph *listened* to their plea.

Again, in Genesis 43, when the brothers returned to Egypt (following the instructions Joseph had given them during their first trip to secure provisions), Joseph *listened* to them.

And again, in Genesis 44, after devising a way to assess his brothers' motives and attitude, he *listened* to them.

And finally, in Genesis 45, Joseph revealed to them his true identity. (See Genesis 42-45.)

Too many people today blurt out what is on their mind before listening to what is being communicated to them or requested of them. Champions learn to *listen first* (and, at that, to first listen to *God*) before responding.

2: Champions Plan

Let Pharaoh look for a discerning and wise man and put him in charge of the land of Egypt. Let Pharaoh appoint commissioners over the land to take a fifth of the harvest of Egypt during the seven years of abundance. They should collect all the food of these good years that are coming and store up the grain under the authority of Pharaoh, to be kept in the cities for food. This food should be held in reserve for the country, to be used during the seven years of famine that will come upon Egypt, so that the country may not be ruined by the famine (Genesis 41:33-36 NIV).

After Joseph interpreted Pharaoh's dream, in Genesis 41:33-36 he then laid out a detailed plan to spare Egypt from a famine that was going to ravage the earth in seven years and would last for seven years. He was able to conceive a precise and intelligent plan because of his experience as manager of the household of Pharaoh's chief of palace security, captain Potiphar. Joseph applied his experience and his knowledge in his plan to help Pharaoh spare Egypt.

3: CHAMPIONS MANAGE SUCCESS

As a result of the plan Joseph laid out for Pharaoh, and the fact that Joseph had gained the wisdom and experience needed to deal with crises, he was chosen by Pharaoh as the man to manage the famine crisis. In order to accomplish this, Pharaoh appointed Joseph as the second most powerful person in Egypt and put him in charge of implementing and overseeing the plan to avert disaster for the nation.

Then Pharaoh said to Joseph, "Inasmuch as God has shown you all this, there is no one as discerning and wise as you. You shall be over my house, and all my people shall be ruled according to your word; only in regard to the throne will I be greater than you." And Pharaoh said to Joseph, "See, I have set you over all the land of Egypt." Then Pharaoh took his signet ring off his hand and put it on Joseph's hand; and he clothed him in garments of fine linen and put a gold chain around his neck. And he had him ride in the second chariot which he had; and they cried out before him, "Bow the knee!" So he set him over all the land of Egypt. Pharaoh also said to Joseph, "I am Pharaoh, and without your consent no man may lift his hand or foot in all the land of Egypt" (Genesis 41:39-44 NKJV).

4: CHAMPIONS PROVIDE

Now, fast-forward to Genesis, Chapter 45. Joseph is the man. Second in command over all of Egypt. He came up with a plan to save the nation from famine and devastation. God had given him the vision to prepare the country to thrive through seven years of famine and a plan to lead them through the crisis of those lean years. He is now managing Egypt, steering the nation toward the fat times. He is their champion, a national hero.

When Joseph's brothers went to Pharaoh to seek grain to get them through the famine, they had not seen Joseph in years. In fact, when they were led before the king's right-hand man, they didn't even recognize that he was their brother, because Joseph had grown up and become not just a man, but an Egyptian ruler. In their wildest imagination, Joseph's brothers wouldn't have expected to see their brother in the palace of Pharaoh as the number one senior official in the land. They figured little Joseph was long dead.

Imagine Joseph's surprise seeing bowing before him the brothers who'd tried to kill him years earlier by tossing him down a well and then selling him into slavery! Yet, here is what Joseph did: *he provided for them.* He made sure they got all the grain they needed to weather the famine; and he even eventually brought his entire family to live in Egypt (see Gen. 42:25; 44:1; 45:3-7).

Let me give you a little footnote: champions do not hold grudges. There are some people who knew you back in the day who had already made up their minds about where you would end up and what you would be doing. Somewhere down the line you're going to run into those people again. And when they see the blessing of the Lord upon your life, when they see the champion you have become, many of them won't even recognize you. If they come to you for help, don't hold a grudge, don't remind them of what they did to you, don't gloat over your success. Simply *help them.* (See Proverbs 24:17.)

Champions forgive. One of many words of wisdom my mother gave me had to do with forgiveness. I had an argument with the girl I was dating and she and I weren't speaking. Out of the clear blue, a few days later she invited me to a party. I told my mother that going to that party was the last thing I would do. My mother, wise sage that she was, said, "Son, don't make it so hard for people to apologize. Inviting you to this party is her way of saying she is sorry." That didn't really go over too well with me at the moment, but I later learned the timeless truth: champions do not bear resentments.

5: CHAMPIONS BLESS

Then his brothers also went and fell down before his face, and they said, "Behold, we are your servants." Joseph said to them,

"Do not be afraid, for am I in the place of God? But as for you, you meant evil against me; but God meant it for good, in order to bring it about as it is this day, to save many people alive. Now therefore, do not be afraid; I will provide for you and your little ones." And he comforted them and spoke kindly to them (Genesis 50:18-21 NKJV).

If you want to be a champion, bless somebody else. Pass on the blessing. Don't be in it just for yourself. Never go through life just to get your own goodies. Every door that you walk through, leave a foot in that door for somebody else coming after you. Leave the door cracked, because you never know when you may have to reach back and bring somebody else in. Just as importantly, you never know when, with hat in hand, you yourself might come before a Joseph you once knew who is now sitting up in high position.

There will be people along your journey in life who will try to discourage you. There will be people on your path who will not even try to understand your vision. There will be those along the way who will try to stop you and block your progress. You do not have time to get bitter. You never read about Joseph whining or complaining about what his brothers did to him. In fact, the next time he saw them, years after they'd dumped him down a well and then sold him to the Ishmaelites for twenty shekels of silver (see Gen. 37:28), he *blessed them*, because he knew that what they meant for evil, God had turned into good.

Throughout his life, Joseph knew that the Champion of all blessings was God. Joseph even told his brothers that it was not they who had sold him off to the Ishmaelites many years earlier, but *God*. He told them in Genesis 45:7-8, "And God sent me before you to preserve you a posterity in the earth, and to save your lives by a great deliverance. So now it was not you that sent me hither, but God: And he hath made me a father to Pharaoh, and lord of all his house, and a ruler throughout all the land of Egypt" (Gen. 45:7-8).

CHAMPIONS HAVE HEART

When Joseph's brothers saw that their father was dead, they said, "Perhaps Joseph will hate us, and may actually repay us for all the evil which we did to him." So they sent messengers to Joseph, saying, "Before your father died he commanded, saying, 'Thus you shall say to Joseph: I beg you, please forgive the trespass of your brothers and their sin; for they did evil to you.' Now, please, forgive the trespass of the servants of the God of your father." And Joseph wept when they spoke to him (Genesis 50:15-17 NKJV).

In Genesis, chapter 50, Joseph's brothers expect to be rejected by him, because Jacob had died and the brothers were fully aware of all the evil things they had done to Joseph when he was a lad. They surmise that now that their father is dead, perhaps out of grief, powerful Joseph might now punish them for what they did.

So they relay the message from their dying father Jacob, asking Joseph to forgive his brothers for the sins and wrongs they had committed in treating him so badly. When Joseph heard that his father had told his brothers to ask for forgiveness, as they threw themselves before him and declared themselves his servants, Joseph *wept*. Here he is, the chief operating officer of the mighty Egyptian empire. The national hero. Tough guy. Sharp businessman. Leader of the people through a devastating world crisis. About to become champion of the budding Jewish nation. Yet, *he had a tender heart.* He wept. (See Genesis 50.)

Want to be a champion? Stay balanced. *Have heart.*

Occasionally I get together with old college friends and we'll get to talking about the usual things. *Where is so-and-so? What ever happened to such-and-such? Have you heard about what's-his-name?* Inevitably, the name of a very prominent national figure I went to school with will come up in the conversation. We used to party together. He was a member of Kappa Alpha Psi, I was a member of Alpha Phi Alpha. The man was brilliant. He became a multimillionaire. But every time any of my classmates talk about him, they all have exactly the same thing to say: that the man had become callous, cold, insensitive, and even cruel over the years. Joseph was yesterday's equivalent of this man. Yet Joseph had heart; he stayed balanced. He was the ruler and national hero and still had a tender heart. He was still a regular guy. He still had his feet on the ground and his head on his shoulders. He could still be touched.

Champions bless. Champions handle success *God's way.* They learn to handle setbacks, because they know that every setback is a setup for a step-up. So manage your relationships. Be a channel of success. When you receive it, pass it on. Sow into somebody else's life. Pour into somebody else's dream, into another person's vision, other people's success. Encourage those around you. When you come across people who mean to do you evil, know that, just as Joseph discovered, God has a way of turning things around and setting you up for success, so that you can then display for them the champion in you.

ENDNOTES

1. For a clear and complete examination of God's Word on money and financial affairs, I refer you to my book *Making Your Money Count: Why We Have It—How to Manage It* (Regal Books, 2007).

2. The word used in the text for *bow* or *fall down and worship* is pesw\n.

Chapter 10

No Overnight Champions

"Actually, I'm an overnight success, but it took twenty years."

—Monty Hall

I am always amazed at how often Hollywood and the media depict someone as an overnight success. And in nearly every case, you discover that the "overnight success" has been paying their dues for a long time. There seems to be almost no concept in today's culture that there is simply no instant success. Here is why: success is the product of *work*. I know that four-letter word causes a problem for many people. But you cannot become a champion without work. Find someone who has been, or who is, a true champion, and I will show you someone who has worked at it, who has put in time and energy, who, on one level or another, got themselves prepared to achieve.

In a previous chapter we looked at Ecclesiastes 9:10, which tells us to do with all our might whatever it is that we do. In other words, you have to work at it. You cannot be successful in anything if you're not willing to pay the price. This is a fundamental and elementary truth. Yet, it is puzzling how many people either do not seem to know that, or they overlook it, or they simply disregard it. But the fact is, success demands persistence as much as becoming a champion requires consistence. Whatever your endeavor is, whatever your goal, your target, your destiny, it must be done with all of your focus and energy. Because there is a direct correlation between the amount of time you put into becoming all you can be and the results you will achieve. I'm not talking about the fact that you may have to work a night and a day job to make ends meet. I'm talking about giving your full attention to that which you have chosen as your life's work.

Life is not a dress rehearsal. We only get one shot to get it right.

For in death, where you are going, there is no working or planning, or knowing, or understanding (Ecclesiastes 9:10 TLB).

This Scripture cuts right to the chase: after you're dead, that's it. When it's over, it's over. You won't spend eternity correcting how you lived. You will spend eternity based on how you lived while you were here. Time is preparation for eternity. That statement is significant because many people—even after making the decision to work at becoming successful in a given area—are guilty of terminal procrastination. They put their goals on time delay. They do it when they get around to it.

A young lady once approached me and said, "I've always wanted to go back to college. But I'm too old now." She was forty at the time. She said, "If I start school right now, it will take me four years to finish. I'd be forty-four years old when I finish. It's too late. I can't do it. I put it off too long."

I said, "My dear, in four years you'll be forty-four years old whether you go to school or not. The question is, will you be forty-four with that degree or without it?"

Many people are guilty of procrastinating, delaying, putting it off—until it's too late. Champions do not procrastinate. If you can put your destiny on hold, then it's probably *not your destiny*. If you can cool down the flames of your passion, then it may not be a passion. It might just be heartburn. It may be a sugar rush from too much chocolate. Might be too much sitting around dreaming.

What many people mistake as their passion or destiny is often simply an expression of someone else's passion or destiny. They see what someone else is doing and they assume it would be a nice thing for them to do too. But if years have gone by since their stated intention to pursue the passion, and they've made no significant strides to bring it to fruition, then it probably wasn't really a passion at all.

Passion keeps you in the fight; it anchors you to God's promise that you will achieve that which you desire as you move in His ways on the path He has ordained for you. You succeed in your passions because you put in the time and energy to bring those passions to life. I'm not talking about hobbies. I'm not talking about a vocation. I'm talking about destinies and calls.

CHAMPIONS INVEST THE TIME

The race is not to the swift or the battle to the strong, nor does food come to the wise or wealth to the brilliant or favor to the learned; but time and chance happen to them all (Ecclesiastes 9:11 NIV).

Ecclesiastes 9:11 suggests two things: success demands work, and work takes *time*.

If you question corporate executives about how they made it to the top, nearly every one of them will tell you that somewhere back in their lives they worked in the mail room, or as the low guy in the sales or accounting department or some low-scale menial job. Ask any successful actor and you'll discover that somewhere along the way that individual was doing summer stock work in front of tiny audiences in some little town somewhere, or had gone on hundreds of casting calls only to get a small bit part. We all know the illustration of the tortoise and the hare, which demonstrates that the winner of the race is not always the swiftest, but the steadiest, the one who consistently plods forward through all obstacles. *Success takes time.*

I'm always baffled by young pastors who come from all over the country to visit Faithful Central Bible Church, mistakenly thinking for some reason that it sprang up overnight. There was a kid once, fresh out of seminary who came to find out how our church had happened so quickly. Bless his heart; he meant no harm. But there is, in this fast-food, instamatic generation, a tendency to factor out the element of the time it takes to become a champion. I am honored to stand before several thousand people every week, but for the most part, the people in the congregation don't realize that there was a time when we held church services with twelve, fifteen people. We didn't start off in a major southern California sports arena. You don't start with a huge crowd. There's a time element to consider. There's a thing called *paying one's dues*.

I know a very gifted young pastor who was often heard saying the Lord would do a "quick work" in his church. He was declaring that his church would grow quickly. Now don't get me wrong; the brother is doing well. In fact he has probably grown faster than the average church, but he is learning that you still have to learn the same lessons along the way—and it's hard to learn patience when you are supposed to be moving quickly. I'll say it again: there are no shortcuts to success! And what looks like a shortcut is usually a dead-end street!

A preacher once said, "Every preacher ought to learn how to preach to empty seats, because at one time or another, you will do it." Success demands work, and success demands time. And God is worth both. Besides, it won't work any other way.

Therefore humble yourselves under the mighty hand of God, that He may exalt you in due time (1 Peter 5:6 NKJV).

There's a subtle revelation in Ecclesiastes 9:11. Where it says, "The race is not to the swift," it means that if you're going to be successful, you cannot run the race comparing yourself with the pace of your opponent. One of the most discouraging things that can completely trip you up is if you begin to watch someone else's career and use that as your own model. *Inspiration*, yes. Imitation, no. To put your mind and your attention on what is happening in someone else's life will throw you off course. Because it is not about the person who got the part you wanted, or who got the promotion before you did. It's about the track and the pace that God is moving *your* life.

If you put your attention on the people and the persons in your life who are swifter than you or more experienced than you or more connected than you, it may discourage you and you might fade back or quit; and that could hamper God's design for your life, because the race indeed is *not* necessarily won by the fastest or the swiftest.

God often places people in the life of a champion for inspiration—and that's all good and well, but don't let another person's accomplishments distract you from your path. To put it in another context, some of the most miserable single people I know are those who see other people getting married and start feeling like they should bend to their biological clock and do something quick.

Champions do not succumb to a temptation to run their lives at someone else's pace. You might be a modern-day equivalent of Abraham or Sarah, who had to wait until they were old enough to be grandparents until they finally had their own child. But that son Isaac led the lineage to the creation of the nation of Israel and directly to the Messiah (see Gen. 16 and 17). However, before Sarah conceived Isaac, she and Abraham decided to rush things, and Abraham fathered a child with Sarah's Egyptian maidservant Hagar. That illegitimate child Ishmael led the lineage to the creation of the Arab nations. And to this day, the Jews and the Arabs are at odds with each other.

Champions do not move in their own timing, but in God's alone.

Ecclesiastes 9:11 says that "time and chance happen to them all." In other words, while time is a factor to building a champion, chance is also an element—not as in a roll of the dice, but as it relates to *providence*. This means that there is not only an element of timing, but also the element of being in the right place. Being in the right place at the right time is not chance or happenstance. What might seem to be "chance," what might seem to be "accident," is actually the providential hand of God, who long ago placed those elements at the ready. God's providence moving behind the scenes is when He positions you in a place that leads you to another place, and had you not been in the first place, you would have never made it to the second place.

God plans each move on the chessboard of life light-years in advance. The dominoes tumble in the manner He ordains—and I guarantee you, He ordains the tumble in favor of those who invest time at His feet.

I am very hesitant sometimes about young preachers who say they've been called to preach yet don't seem to understand that if indeed the Lord has called them to the pulpit, then they've also been called to take the time to prepare. When a young preacher approaches me and says, "Pastor, I have been called to preach," they are always taken aback by my response. I generally say to them, "We'll see. We'll see." Because at some point the question arises, "When are you going to work on this and make it truly the priority of your life? When are you going to shift gears and rearrange things in your life to reflect what you said God told you to do?"

This may sound like a harsh word, but I want to suggest to you that if your mind and efforts are not consistently active in the pursuit of the call of God on your life, then *you are ignoring God.*

Nothing is accomplished by accident; time is always an element. A period of work and preparation is crucial to developing the champion in you.

Be patient, then, brothers, until the Lord's coming. See how the farmer waits for the land to yield its valuable crop and how patient he is for the autumn and spring rains. You too, be patient and stand firm (James 5:7-8 NIV).

CHAMPIONS DEAL WITH REJECTION

Champions don't passively wait around for someone to give them a break. They don't wait for the phone to ring. And they don't wilt when they're told "no." For example, if you're looking to move up in your career, then blast out your resume to prospective employers, make follow-up phone calls, and keep pushing forward, no matter how bad the economy or overcrowded the field. Eventually, if nothing else, the law of averages will catch up with your efforts and you will land that position. Champions aren't thin-skinned. *Keep at it.* Don't quit. That one-hundredth "no" might be the one just before the big "yes."

Recently I came across a reality television program where they were auditioning singers for a band. A man announced to the hopeful candidates, "Let me tell you up front: if you cannot handle rejection, you're in the wrong place. Maybe you need to check yourself, because if negativity throws you off that much, then you're barking up the wrong tree."

We were told "no" over twenty times when we approached financial institutions about our serious interest in purchasing the Great Western Forum. It almost felt like everybody had talked to everybody else and agreed among themselves that when we walked in the door, the standard answer would be "no" to Faithful Central Bible Church. We were told "no" so often that it almost started to feel like a conspiracy. Some people were very creative and sophisticated with their *no*s, too. Others just flat said *no*—they weren't going to help us, guide us, advise us, loan us, talk to us. They were telling us "no" so often that in one meeting I felt like saying "no" *for* the man we were asking. I was even getting "no" from people who were supposed to be involved in the deal on our side!

I learned to tune out the "you can'ts" and analyze the "no ways." I would adjust my approach for the next presentation and beef up what was weak from the last time around. By the time we finally got to the final presentation, everything we had was tight, because everything had been under intense scrutiny by many people for months. And in the end, we had a sharp, well-honed presentation.

EXAMINE THE NEGATIVE

It is wise to closely examine what is behind some of the "nos" you will get. For example, if you sense that God told you in the midnight hour that He is going to use your voice all over the world as a great diva, but you can't carry a tune in a bucket with a lid on it, and Momma tells you that you can't sing, your husband tells you that you can't sing, your best friend tells you that you can't sing, and the guy running the board at the recording studio you rented to cut a song demo tells you that you can't sing…well, my friend, odds are you probably can't sing.

At some point, it is just plain common sense to analyze the negativity, because there is often important revelation in rejection. There are times when what appears to be negative can actually be positive and helpful input if you are willing to examine it with an open mind. The champion uses wisdom in looking at an issue from many reasonable perspectives. It's always possible that if you tighten up your act, improve the weak areas, get more educated, take more lessons, then next time around you might just blow them out of the water with your singing. Or your running. Or your cooking. Or your violin playing.

Sometimes you have to remind yourself of the answer to the old question, "How do you get to Carnegie Hall?" *Practice, practice, practice!*

CHAMPIONS SHAKE THE DUST OFF THEIR FEET

But whatever house you enter, first say, "Peace to this house." And if a son of peace is there, your peace will rest on it; if not, it will return to you. And remain in the same house, eating and drinking such things as they give, for the laborer is worthy of his wages. Do not go from house to house. Whatever city you enter, and they receive you, eat such things as are set before you. And heal the sick there, and say to them, "The kingdom of God has come near to you." But whatever city you enter, and they do not receive you, go out into its streets and say, "The very dust of your city which clings to us we wipe off against you. Nevertheless know this, that the kingdom of God has come near you" (Luke 10:5-11 NKJV).

In Luke 10, Jesus gave instructions to the seventy He was sending out by twos ahead of Him to every town and place where He was about to go. He basically told them, "I have destined you to be an extension of the Kingdom. When you go into a house or to a city or to a place and they receive you, then bless them. Minister there. Serve there. But if you go into a place that will not receive you, then shake the dust off your feet" (see Luke 10:5-11). In today's vernacular He might have said, "Hit the road if they just won't have you." The idea is that if you go into a house or to a city that does not receive you, then move on down the road, because somebody further along your path will receive you.

The Kingdom of God is still going to come whether people accept it or not. This applies to the champion seeking to fulfill his or her destiny. The will of God will not be stopped just because someone else did not agree with it. This is not a spirit of arrogance, it is a spirit of confidence. At some point you've got to realize that even when you've been turned down, in God's greater scheme of things, your rejection today does not end your journey. It simply means that in some situations with some people you must shake the dust off your feet. If they won't receive you, don't trip out, don't freak out, don't check out. Just know that somewhere else down the line there will be someone who will appreciate what you have to offer, how talented you are, and what gifts the Lord gave you.

Jesus let the seventy know that He had prepared people who were going to receive them. Not everybody was going to receive them, so they shouldn't give up when they were turned away; they were to just keep moving forward, because people *were* going to receive them.

You may have sensed the same wall of rejection in your life, perhaps when you went for an interview and the person who interviewed you talked to the person you spoke with the previous time and they agreed in advance that they weren't going to hire you. Here is some "straight talk," one Christian to another: once you realize what God has called you to do, once you are determined to do what He has ordained for you, don't let "no" stop you. Champions learn how to shake off rejection. Don't let obstacles stop you. Don't let hurdles stop you. Don't let rejection stop you. Don't let negativity stop you. Tune them out.

Don't hang around people who really don't want to see you advance the Kingdom of God. Don't spend too much close, personal time with folks who rain on your parade and try to burst your bubble. Negativity and rejection are just a part of the game. For the champion, rejection is not a stop sign, it's a bump in the road to success. Shrug it off. If you can't take it, you can't make it. So step up your game a notch or two and go back at it.

CHAMPIONS WORK SMARTER

If the axe is dull and he does not sharpen its edge, then he must exert more strength. Wisdom has the advantage of giving success (Ecclesiastes 10:10 NASB).

Success requires that you work hard, but it also requires that you work smart. Ecclesiastes 10:10 is the picture of a man trying to cut down a tree, but he's doing it with a dull axe. So he decides to swing his axe harder, when the wiser move would be to *sharpen the axe.*

Champions don't try to chop through their forests with a dull axe. If, for example, you graduated from college with a bachelor's degree three years ago, and your goal was to go into corporate management, but you haven't even landed a job, you could have earned an MBA by now. Maybe you're hitting the tree with a blunt blade.

Faithful Central Bible Church is located in Southern California, land of a million future movie stars. Once, a young lady called my office and said, "I'm coming to Hollywood, and I want to go into the movies and be a star."

"Take a number and stand in the line," I told her, "because just about everybody who comes to L.A. wants to become a movie star." Or actor, writer, director, dancer, singer, choreographer, cinematographer. Los Angeles is star heaven.

Okay, fine, so she wants to be a star. She said she's coming to Hollywood to go to a casting call. But her resume indicated that all she had done was appear in her high school production of *Little Red Riding Hood*. The last few people I had heard from who also came to Hollywood to go to casting calls in hopes of becoming stars had collectively done four videos, three television commercials, and one independent, low-budget movie—and not one of them had gotten the part they were hoping to get.

The young lady who had sought my input didn't get the part either. She simply had not prepared herself to run with the pros. She showed up at a gunfight with a butter knife. She had hit the tree with a dull axe.

We've all done the same thing at one time or another. This is a little embarrassing to admit, but when Faithful Central Bible Church decided to pursue purchasing the Forum and using the sports arena as a for-profit business when church services were not being held, I thought you just went into some bank and told somebody, "Good morning, ma'am. We're going to start a business here, and we want to buy the Great Western Forum, recent home of the Lakers."

The first thing they said was, "O*kaaay*. Where's your business plan?"

I said, "Well, give me a minute. Let me write something up for you real quick."

I was so embarrassed. The people with me said, "No, no, Bishop. That won't get it. We need a *real* business plan."

It's amazing how people won't know you're not prepared if you don't say anything. Sometimes it's best just to sit there and look smart (it's the old saying: *it's better to be silent and be thought a fool than to open your mouth and remove all doubt!*). I was surprised at how much we didn't know about what we were attempting to do with that multimillion-dollar purchase. The documents alone for the final purchase of the arena seemed to be about four-feet thick. I am not kidding. We had a room full of tables with nothing on them but documents. We had so many documents to sign, I had to hire people to read them for me because there were so many details involved. When we signed them, we had to go table by table, row by row, in a room full of documents.

I had a good vision for the enterprise; I was very clear about what we wanted to accomplish and about the vision God had given us. But what I did not know was that at some point I was trying to hit a big tree with a dull axe. I didn't understand back then how to sharpen myself on what it would take to successfully close such a huge deal. But I definitely learned along the way.

It's not simply about working harder; it's about sharpening your axe. Sharpening the axe has to do with gathering more information and being more up-to-date. It's about having a clear and informed understanding of what it takes to succeed. Becoming a success is not about knowledge; it's about *wisdom*. Ecclesiastes 10:10 says, "If the ax is dull, and one does not sharpen the edge, then he must use more strength; but wisdom brings success" (Eccles. 10:10 NKJV). It is not knowledge that brings success. It's *wisdom*.

The difference between wisdom and knowledge is that knowledge is the accumulation of information and facts. It's what you *know*. You have a *knowledge* of a business. You have a *knowledge* of the steps that it takes to build something. But the Ecclesiastes verse does not say that knowledge brings success. The text says that it is *wisdom* that brings success. Knowledge is the accumulation of information and facts, while wisdom is the *utilization of the information* acquired. Knowledge is what you know; wisdom is how you use and handle what you know.

That's why smart people can fail. I know people who have much more knowledge than I have (such as the experts involved in our church's purchase of the Forum). And I also know that smart people don't necessarily have the wisdom required to pull off and sustain a great accomplishment (such as the knowledgeable people who said it wouldn't work for a church to purchase and run a large sports arena).

A pastor friend of mine in Los Angeles went to school for many years to get a Doctor of Ministry degree. He took classes in church growth, leadership, pastoral ministry, and other relevant courses to pastoring and leading a church. In addition, he often went to conferences and conventions on preaching, pastoring, and leadership. He received very good grades and was well known around the campus as a good student with a desire to lead the people of God. This man had all of the information and knowledge and facts about how to grow a church ministry. He did eventually receive a Doctor of Ministry degree. Now, please don't take this observation as a criticism, but nearly 30 years later, the church he organized has fewer than a hundred people in it. He probably sees about 40 or 50 people on a Sunday.

Please don't interpret this as judgmental. I'm trying to make the point that here is a man who had the knowledge, passed all the tests, got *A*'s in every class, earned his doctorate, became a pastor, and now has only a few dozen people in a church that is decades old. If you take that anecdote as a judgmental statement, then you will miss the point: succeeding at bringing to fruition God's call on your life is *not* all about knowledge or learning or intelligence or connections. The Bible says that it is *wisdom* that brings success.

THE SOURCE OF WISDOM

The LORD possessed me [wisdom] at the beginning of His way, before His works of old. I have been established from everlasting, from the beginning, before there was ever an earth (Proverbs 8:22-23 NKJV).

So now you're eager to work, you recognize God's call on your life, you're willing to put in the time, you recognize that it does not happen overnight, you've gathered information to sharpen your axe, and you realize that it's not just information but wisdom that brings success. So where does wisdom come from? Knowledge comes from books, experience, classes, discussions, mentoring, etc.—that's knowledge. For the source, function, and use of wisdom, let's go first to the book of James:

> *If any of you lacks wisdom, let him ask of God, who gives to all liberally and without reproach, and it will be given to him* (James 1:5 NKJV).

According to James 1:5, wisdom comes from God. Knowledge, facts, and information can come from a book, from the Internet, from classes. But how you *handle* that information, how you deal with truth, how you respond to facts, and how they relate to your destiny, your call, and your passion, requires wisdom. And wisdom comes *only* from God. Wisdom is God-given insight and instruction in the practicalities of life. Knowledge involves principles; wisdom is about practice. I know pastors who never set foot in a seminary. I know leaders who never darkened the doors of a college. I know successful men and women who never graced the hallowed ivy-covered walls of famed academic institutions. But they are champions because they operated more out of wisdom than traditional knowledge and the common practices of the day.

Wisdom, and the realization of the need for wisdom, is part of a process. For the full process, let's look at the verses that immediately precede James 1:5…

> *My brethren, count it all joy when you fall into various trials, knowing that the testing of your faith produces patience. But let*

patience have its perfect work, that you may be perfect and complete, lacking nothing (James 1:2-4 NKJV).

How do you handle these "various trials" (which the King James Version calls "divers [diverse] temptations") (see James 1:2)? How do you handle rejection? How do you handle obstacles? Champions handle them with wisdom. If you lack wisdom, you ask God for it.

Here is the James 1 flow of wisdom as it relates to God's purpose for His champions:

First, by faith you receive your vision from God, and you prepare yourself to step into your destiny. If you lack wisdom in preparing yourself, ask God and He will give it to you, so you can go around obstacles and start to grow as a champion.

Next, as you move forward in your vision, your faith will be tested by various trials, which will produce patience within you. If you lack wisdom in responding to the challenges to your faith, ask God and He will give it to you, so your faith will remain unshaken as you continue walking in your destiny and growing as a champion.

And finally, once patience has perfected its work in you, you will be complete, lacking *nothing*.

Let's look at it through the example of God's call to Abraham. First, Abraham is given his vision:

I will make you a great nation; I will bless you and make your name great; and you shall be a blessing. I will bless those who bless you, and I will curse him who curses you; and in you all the families of the earth shall be blessed (Genesis 12:2-3 NKJV).

God told Abraham that He was going to bless his children and bless the world through him. Abraham told God he didn't have any children. God told him He would give him children and that they would be blessed. That was Abraham's revelation from God. He received it by faith.

Then came Abraham's test. When champions get the call from God, just as they received it by faith, their readiness to step out in faith will then be tested. I promise you, it is *guaranteed* that your faith *will* (not "maybe," not "probably," not "you have a pretty good chance," but it *will*) *be tested*. Once you determine that God has called you to do something, it will be tested and you will be required to respond in the affirmative. Whether it's buying a building, starting a new career, going into the mission field, or whatever it is, after receiving the vision, God will test your faith. Because if Abraham is called the "Father of the Faithful" and his faith was tested, then we as champions should also expect to be tested. [1]

Now it came to pass after these things that God tested Abraham, and said to him, "Abraham!" And he said, "Here I am" (Gen. 22:1 NKJV).

Follow closely now, because the test of Abraham was a particularly supreme test: God was going to try Abraham's faith by having him do something that God Himself prohibited: the blood sacrifice of a human being...

Then He said, "Take now your son, your only son Isaac, whom you love, and go to the land of Moriah, and offer him there as a

burnt offering on one of the mountains of which I shall tell you"
(Genesis 22:2 NKJV).

What did Abraham, that patriarch of the nation of Israel and
father of the faithful, do? He did not gasp in shock. He did not
whine or grovel or argue or moan. He did not lecture God that
human sacrifice was against God's own ways. He saddled up. He
rose early in the morning, took two of his young men, along with
his son Isaac, the kindling wood, and the knife he was instructed to
plunge into his young boy, and he did exactly what God told him
to do—with no deviations this time. No advice from Sarah. No
nighttime visit to Hagar. He mounted up.

Abraham passed his test of faith so resoundingly that when his
little entourage reached the place in the land of Moriah where God
had indicated the sacrifice of Isaac was to take place, read what
Abraham told his servants as he was about to leave to take his only
son to the spot where he would then thrust the blade into the child:

*Abraham said to his young men, "Stay here with the donkey; the
lad and I will go yonder and worship, and **we will come back to
you.**"...But Isaac spoke to Abraham his father and said, "My
father!" And he said, "Here I am, my son." Then he said, "Look,
the fire and the wood, but where is the lamb for a burnt offering?" And Abraham said, "My son, **God will provide for
Himself the lamb for a burnt offering**"* (Genesis 22:5,7-8
NKJV).

"*We* will come back to you," said Abraham to his servants; and,
"*God will provide for Himself the lamb* for the burnt offering," he

told Isaac (Gen. 22:5). By this time in his life, Abraham's faith in God had become so rock solid and set deep and honed sharp that the old sage knew that he would be coming back *with a live Isaac.* He knew that God had promised him descendants as numerous as the sands of the ocean through his only son Isaac. He knew that God abhorred human sacrifice. Therefore, Abraham must have reasoned that, after he sacrificed Isaac according to God's instructions, God might then either raise Isaac from the dead (see Heb. 11:19) or change His instructions at the last moment. Or, at the very least, make a brand-new Isaac.

Abraham knew what God could do. He was ready to put in the knife at God's merest command. And as it turned out, God stayed Abraham's hand and indeed provided an offering, a ram that had gotten its horns caught in a nearby thicket (see Gen. 22:13).

Throughout the test, Abraham patiently did as God instructed.

A patient man has great understanding (Proverbs 14:29 NIV).

A champion's faith in God is rock solid. As James 1:3 states, when our faith is tested, it will produce patience. If the testing of your faith does not produce patience, then you're probably being tested in the wrong course of your life. And it might be an indication that you're following the wrong destiny or that you're on the wrong track. In other words, when the Bible says your faith will be tested and that the result of that testing will be patience, it is referring to an attitude that says, "I know what God said, and I'm not going to give up on what He said will come to pass, no matter how tough it gets, no matter how long it takes. I'm going to hang in here until I see the day of His blessing."

James 1:4 says, "But let patience have its perfect work, that you may be perfect and complete, lacking nothing" (James 1:4 NKJV). When your faith is tested—when you are told "no," when you're rejected, declined, doors closed in your face, phone calls not returned, resume tossed in the round file—that testing of your faith produces in you the patience and the ability to endure under the pressure, knowing that the problems will not last. Letting patience have its perfect work then produces perfection (or maturity), so that you will then lack nothing.

"Its perfect work" can be pictured in the analogy of a woman carrying a baby that is coming to full term. If the testing of your faith does not produce patience, then you run the risk of aborting the "baby of destiny." In other words, if you let the test throw you off and you drop out of the race, if you let the test discourage you to the point where you throw away your destiny, then you are choosing to abort the destiny that resides within you.

Champions allow that destiny baby to develop to full term. During its development, the birth pangs produce in them maturity and strength; and when the vision comes forth, success. The challenge is to carry the baby with all of the labor pains and the problems and trials that come with it. That takes wisdom. You need to know from God how to lay, how to stand, how to position yourself, how to eat and nourish yourself properly, what to stay away from and what to put in your body, who to trust, how to dress, where to go—all of those challenges of life once you receive your call from God. You need wisdom to know that you are carrying something within you that God has placed there.

Champions do not give up on their passion, vision, or destiny just because they get a pain here and an ache there. They allow their passion's reality to come to full term, pushing until it comes forth, bringing to fruition that which God has ordained.

The champion's success (seeing the vision of God brought to fulfillment) is about *work*. It's about *time*. It's about *patience*. It's about *wisdom*.

God did not make you to abort your destiny. God made you to be a champion and to succeed in what He ordained for you. The psalmist stated it this way:

> *I will lift up my eyes to the hills—from whence comes my help? My help comes from the LORD, who made heaven and earth. He will not allow your foot to be moved; He who keeps you will not slumber* (Psalm 121:1-3 NKJV).

James 1:5 says it bluntly: "If you lack wisdom, ask God"—just as Moses put it in Deuteronomy:

> *Seek the LORD your God, and you will find Him if you seek Him with all your heart and with all your soul* (Deuteronomy 4:29 NKJV).

Champions pray for wisdom. So pray that God will grant you wisdom. Pray that God would encourage you. Realize that the testing of your faith will bring forth patience. And when patience has come to full term, it will produce maturity and completion and fulfillment.

Pray for God to guide whatever your hands find to do. Start by asking God what He would have you do. Not what looks good. Not what's easy. Not what will make you rich or famous. Ask Him, "What would *You* have me to do, Lord?" You are here for a purpose. You are not to do what Jane is doing or John is doing but what *God* wants *you* to be doing.

What a tragedy it would be to spend your life doing the wrong thing. "Whatever your hand finds to do, do it with your might," Ecclesiastes 9:10 says, "for there is no work or device or knowledge or wisdom in the grave where you are going" (NKJV). It all comes to a stop when you hit the grave. What a tragedy to get to the end and hear God say, "That was not your assignment. Why didn't you come to Me to ask what great and glorious destiny *I* had for you?"

A young lady once called me and said, "It happened to me."

"What?" I asked her.

"It happened to me," she repeated.

"*What* happened to you?" I asked again.

She said, "I turned in a paper at school and got an F." I asked her for some details and she said, "The teacher wrote, 'Good paper, but this was not the assignment.'"

As I said earlier, the exact same thing also once happened to me.

Oh, the tragedy to spend your life and your time and your energy doing the wrong thing. God has given you a gift. God has given you knowledge. God has given you talent. God has given you ability. Wisdom asks, "How will you use it?"

ENDNOTE

1. When the Lord tests us, our failure to follow His command can have devastating results, as shown by the example of the prophet Jonah, whom God told to go preach against Nineveh. Instead, Jonah fled to Tarshish—and got swallowed by a great fish. Or the example of King David, who counted the fighting men (see 2 Sam. 24:10) against God's will, which resulted in three days of plague and 70,000 people dead. Or the example of Moses striking the rock rather than speaking to it (see Num. 20:11), which resulted in him not being allowed to enter the Promised Land. Even champions can fail God's tests, but these examples from antiquity stand as stark reminders to champions today: do as God tells us, or be prepared to suffer consequences.

Chapter 11

Conclusion:
There *Is* a Champion in *You*

---

*Not that I have already attained, or am already perfected; but I
press on, that I may lay hold of that for which Christ Jesus has
also laid hold of me. Brethren, I do not count myself to have
apprehended; but one thing I do, forgetting those things which
are behind and reaching forward to those things which are
ahead, I press toward the goal for the prize of the upward call of
God in Christ Jesus* (Philippians 3:12-14 NKJV).

THROUGH this book I trust that you have come to realize
that there is a champion residing right now inside of you.
You may not think you look like a champion. You may not
feel like much of a champion. But there is one in you, and only you
can choose to take hold of that reality.

You may have experienced defeats, failures, and setbacks along
the path of your life. But those are not what define who you are in
God. It is our responses to our challenges that develop us into the

champions God so desires that we become. You wouldn't be where you are today if you hadn't experienced some trials and tribulations. No one who has not experienced struggles becomes a champion. A person's worth is built, refined, and tested in the fire of life's trials.

You have been recruited and handpicked by God for *His* team. He didn't choose you for who you are, but for who you can become. When He looks at you, He sees a winner. He sees what you were created to be and to do. He sees the destiny of the champion in you. But your championship cannot emerge until you *get in the game*. It's your choice: stand on the sidelines and watch real life pass by (as too many Christians do), or join God's team, take the field, and start racking up victories for the Lord.

CHAMPIONS STAY THE COURSE AND STAND THEIR GROUND

Once you get in the game, *stay in the game*. See it through. Don't let the team down. The day comes for us each when it's "Game Over," and the champions will hear those words from the Lord: "Well done, good and faithful servant" (Matt. 25:21 NKJV).

Keep faithful on a steady diet of the breakfast of champions, the Word of God. It will strengthen you through rough times and will sustain you during the good. Keep your eyes on the prize: the glorification of Jesus.

A few years ago a young man named Mike Delcavo competed against 127 other runners in the Division 2 NCAA cross-country championship at the University of California in Riverside. During the 10,000-meter race, Delcavo began lagging to about the middle of the pack. Then, about halfway through the race, the leader made a wrong turn, and scores of runners behind him blindly followed him. Delcavo, however, realized what had happened, stayed on the correct course, and even tried to urge the runners around him to follow him. He was able to convince only four other men to go his way—the right way. Delcavo finished first, simply because he chose not to follow the crowd. He had prepared in advance. He knew the path. He stayed the course.

Champions recognize and choose the right path, even though it may not be the popular path with everyone else. It's like the Robert Frost poem *The Road Not Taken*. In the poem, two roads diverged in the woods. The first road was well worn by the number of travelers who had taken it on their journeys. The other road was rarely used and had become overgrown with foliage and tall grass. As the traveler happened upon the two roads, he pondered over which road he should take. The obvious choice wasn't the one he ended up making. He took the road less traveled, and in the end, it made all the difference to his journey.

God's road is not widely traveled by the majority of people in the world today. Sadly, not even most people who call themselves Christians truly and closely follow God's narrow path. But God is watching us each and all.

Champions almost always take the less obvious, seemingly unrecognizable path, usually because few dare to tread that way. God's ways are not those generally followed by men. His thinking is not like ours. He does not tend to take easy paths of least resistance. His blade swings at the farthest edges of the dense forest, as He clears a path for His children to safely follow...*if* they choose to follow Him.

Join with others in following my example, brothers, and take note of those who live according to the pattern we gave you. For, as I have often told you before and now say again even with tears, many live as enemies of the cross of Christ. Their destiny is destruction, their god is their stomach, and their glory is in their shame. Their mind is on earthly things. But our citizenship is in heaven. And we eagerly await a Savior from there, the Lord Jesus Christ (Philippians 3:17-20 NIV).

Winston Churchill, one of the greatest and most notable prime ministers in the history of the United Kingdom, was a champion. Yet, he faced obstacles that could have derailed him from his destiny. For one, he was plagued by a speech impediment (as was Moses). During the darkest days of World War II, he stood his ground against the forces of evil, even remaining resolute in his refusal to negotiate with Germany when the defeat of Britain seemed imminent.

In a speech made to the students of Harrow School in October of 1941, Churchill eloquently heralded the solemn duty of the champion:

"This is the lesson: Never give in, never give in, never, never, never, never—in nothing, great or small, large or petty—never give in except to convictions of honour and good sense. Never yield to force; never yield to the apparently overwhelming might of the enemy."[1]

—Winston Churchill

The heart of a champion beats during the thrill of victory and continues beating even in the agony of defeat. Champions remain constant in whatever situation they find themselves, knowing that they are on a steady road that will eventually lead to the completion of their divine purpose.

There are many champions who will never be pictured on the front page of a newspaper or headlined on the evening news or featured in a book or displayed on the cover of a Wheaties cereal box. Their story will never be told on ESPN or CNN or the BBC or recorded anywhere in the chronicles of history. It is not public recognition that bestows on them the mantle of *champion*. What gives them the right to the title is that they have overcome failure. They have shrugged off rejection by detractors. They have risen above the status quo of average and ordinary, and they have emerged triumphant in the eyes of the only One who counts: Almighty Jehovah God.

During the 1968 Summer Olympics, held in Mexico City's Olympic Stadium, several thousand spectators lingered as the last of the marathoners concluded the 26-mile endurance trek and crossed the finish line. When it appeared that all of the runners had completed the course, the stands began to empty out, when suddenly an ambulance rushed onto the track with sirens blaring. Spectators froze as they saw a solitary runner from the east African coastal nation of Tanzania stagger into the stadium with a leg injury. During the race he had fallen, dislocating and seriously damaging his knee. Yet John Stephen Akhwari had refused to quit. Bloody and bruised, he painstakingly made his way down the track to the thunderous applause of the remaining onlookers in the stands until he stepped over the finish line, last of the seventy-four competitors in the race.

Later, when asked why he had continued running in spite of his injury, Akhwari replied, "My country did not send me to Mexico City to start the race. They sent me to finish."

Though he was the final runner to cross the finish line, he was a champion, because *champions finish the race.*

If you never quit, you will never lose. Run the race marked out for you and go the entire distance. For only then can you join your fellow champions in the winner's circle and receive your reward, proclaiming with a shout the words of the great champion, apostle Paul of Tarsus:

> *I have fought the good fight, I have finished the race, I have kept the faith. From now on there is reserved for me the crown of righteousness, which the Lord, the righteous judge, will give me on that day, and not only to me but also to all who have longed for his appearing* (2 Timothy 4:7-8 NRSV).

Always remember: true champions are made, not born. It is God who builds champions; but He only does it with those who possess a willing spirit.

It has been said that a leader is only a leader if he or she is leading someone, and that success is all about monetary wealth, fame, or power. But champions are in a class all by themselves: they are not defined by whether or not they have many followers, nor by money, nor by fame, nor by power, but by how they conduct themselves, by how they behave in this turbulent and distracting world, by how they live and influence people around them in ways that glorify God and encourage and inspire others ever onward.

It is my sincere hope that this book has offered you relevant examples of the qualities of a true champion today, and how those attributes can be appropriated by anyone who wants to become a real champion in a modern world.

God allows us each to choose whether we want to conform to His image of a champion or to walk to the beat of our own drummer. He will not force the wise decision upon us. Only you can answer the question, "What will you do with the champion in you?"

ENDNOTE

1. Winston S. Churchill, *The Unrelenting Struggle: War Speeches by the Right*, (Boston: Little, Brown & Co., 1942).

About the Author

KENNETH C. Ulmer, PhD, is Senior Pastor of Faithful Central Bible Church in Los Angeles. In 2000 the congregation purchased and now worships in The Great Western Forum, previous home of the Los Angeles Lakers professional basketball team. They also operate the building as a commercial entertainment venue.

Dr. Ulmer is currently President of The King's College and Seminary in Los Angeles. He participated in the study of Ecumenical Liturgy and Worship at Magdalene College at Oxford University in England, and has served as an instructor in Pastoral Ministry and Homiletics at Grace Theological Seminary; as an instructor of African-American Preaching at Fuller Theological Seminary in Pasadena; as an adjunct professor at Biola University (where he served on the Board of Trustees); and as an adjunct professor at Pepperdine University. He also served as a mentor in the Doctor of Ministry degree program at United Theological Seminary in Dayton, Ohio.

Dr. Ulmer received his Bachelor of Arts degree in Broadcasting & Music from the University of Illinois. After accepting his call to the ministry, Dr. Ulmer was ordained at Mount Moriah Missionary Baptist Church in Los Angeles, and shortly afterward founded Macedonia Bible Baptist Church in San Pedro, California. He has studied at Pepperdine University, Hebrew Union College, the University of Judaism and Christ Church, and Wadham College at Oxford University in England. In June 1986, he received a Ph.D. from Grace Graduate School of Theology in Long Beach, California (which became the West Coast Campus of Grace Theological Seminary). He was awarded an Honorary Doctor of Divinity from Southern California School of Ministry, and received his Doctor of Ministry from United Theological Seminary.

Dr. Ulmer is Bishop of Christian Education of the Full Gospel Baptist Church Fellowship, where he sat on the Bishops' Council. He has served on the Board of Directors of The Gospel Music Workshop of America; the Pastor's Advisory Council to the Mayor of the City of Inglewood, California; and the Board of Trustees of Southern California School of Ministry. Dr. Ulmer is the Presiding Bishop over the Macedonia International Bible Fellowship, based in Johannesburg, South Africa, which is an association of pastors representing ministries in Africa and in the U.S.

Dr. Ulmer has written several books, including *A New Thing* (a reflection on the Full Gospel Baptist Movement); *Spiritually Fit to Run the Race* (a guide to godly living); *In His Image: An Intimate Reflection of God* (an update of his book, *The Anatomy of God*); his current bestseller, *Making Your Money Count: Why We Have it— How To Manage it* (featured on "This is Your Day" with Benny Hinn); and *The Champion in You.*

Ministry Website: www.faithfulcentral.com.

OTHER BOOKS BY KENNETH ULMER

Making Your Money Count

Spiritually Fit to Run the Race

A New Thing

In His Image

Notes

Additional copies of this book and other book titles from DESTINY IMAGE are available at your local bookstore.

Call toll-free: 1-800-722-6774.

Send a request for a catalog to:

Destiny Image® Publishers, Inc.
P.O. Box 310
Shippensburg, PA 17257-0310

"Speaking to the Purposes of God for This Generation and for the Generations to Come."

For a complete list of our titles, visit us at www.destinyimage.com.